Sewing a Travel Wardrobe

George Washington Vanderbilt's wife, Edith Stuyvesant Dresser, was an avid photographer at the turn of the century. In this 1906 photograph, she is shown with her tripod and camera on Asheville, NC's Biltmore Estate.

Sewing a Travel Wardrobe

Versatile Clothes & Stylish Accessories for Every Adventure

KATE MATHEWS

LARK BOOKS
A Division of Sterling Publishing Co. Inc.
New York

This book is dedicated to Betty Pecsenye,
professional woman, lifelong world traveler, and my beloved aunt—
for always encouraging me to be curious about everything, and everywhere.

Art Director: Dana Irwin
Photography: Sandra Stambaugh
Illustrations: Bernadette Wolf
Production: Hannes Charen, Dana Irwin

Library of Congress Cataloging-in-Publication Data
Mathews, Kate.
       Sewing a travel wardrobe : versatile clothes & stylish accessories
for every adventure / by Kate Mathews.
            p.   cm.
       Includes index.
       ISBN 1-57990-222-7
       1. Clothing and dress.   2. Travel.   3. Travel paraphernalia.   4. Dress accessories.   I. Title.
TT649.M38   1999
646.4'04—dc21   98-52373
                                                 CIP

10 9 8 7 6 5 4 3 2

Published by Lark Books, a division of
Sterling Publishing Co., Inc.
387 Park Avenue South, New York, N.Y. 10016

© 2000, by Kate Matthews

Distributed in Canada by Sterling Publishing,
c/o Canadian Manda Group, One Atlantic Ave., Suite 105
Toronto, Ontario, Canada M6K 3E7

Distributed in Australia by Capricorn Link (Australia) Pty Ltd.,
P.O. Box 6651, Baulkham Hills, Business Centre
NSW 2153, Australia

Distributed in the U.K. by:
Guild of Master Craftsman Publications Ltd.
Castle Place 166 High Street, Lewes, East Sussex, England, BN7 1XU
Tel: (+ 44) 1273 477374 Fax: (+ 44) 1273 478606
Email: pubs@thegmcgroup.com, Web: www.gmcpublications.com

If you have questions or comments about this book, please contact:
Lark Books, 50 College St., Asheville, NC 28801, (828) 253-0467

Printed in Hong Kong

ISBN 1-57990-222-7

CONTENTS

ACKNOWLEDGMENTS

The author wishes to express heartfelt thanks to all the folks who contributed to this book:

The designers, *for their ingenious sewing ideas and travel fervor.*

The models, *who patiently endured hours of changing clothes, waiting for the next shot, and giving the camera their best smiles: Beth Benischek, Kelly McEnany, Karen John, Charles Pittman, Heather Spencer, Danielle Truscott, and Nicole Tuggle.*

The staff of the Biltmore Estate *in Asheville, North Carolina, and especially Kathleen McArthur Mosher and Laura Brower from Public Relations for their legendary Southern hospitality. They made doors open, lights turn on and off, and problems disappear. They also generously loaned several historic photos that George Vanderbilt brought back from his 1890s travels to Europe. You'll see these photos scattered throughout the book, and more about the Biltmore Estate on page 7.*

Lois and Herb Marsh, *the gracious innkeepers at North Lodge On Oakland (see below), in Asheville, North Carolina, who let us sneak a few hours of photography in their lovely home before guests arrived.*

Sandra Stambaugh, *hard-working photographer, who kept us all on schedule so we wouldn't "lose the light."*

Lisa Sanders, *photo stylist, who always seemed to find the perfect accessory and made sure the models looked their absolute best.*

Debra and Charles Logsdon, *who generously provided their 28-foot Tioga camper for us to use as a model changing room, prop shop, and pit stop.*

Jennifer Hubbell *at Sharon Luggage and* **Sandra Soto**, *for lending their vintage suitcases.*

Joan Baez, Sandra Betzina, Charlotte Lunsford Berry, Kathy Triplett, *and many other seasoned travelers for generously sharing their tips for successful wardrobe planning.*

The globetrotters *who lent their travel photos: Jessi Cinque, Susan Hooper, Todd Kaderabek, Constance Richards, and Patricia Wald.*

Dana Irwin, *art director, who applied her awesome design talents to this and five other of my books with enthusiasm and fresh ideas.*

Carol Taylor, *Lark Books publisher, for her unfailing support, advice, good humor, and encouragement throughout the lengthy voyage from book concept to publication.*

Bob Bowles, *my husband and best friend, for driving the camper during the photo shoot, making sure we all got lunch, and doing all sorts of odd jobs with a winning smile.*

NORTH LODGE ON OAKLAND BED & BREAKFAST

When innkeepers Lois and Herb Marsh lived and worked in England, they spent their weekends traveling the countryside and enjoying the area's bed and breakfast hospitality. Several years later, they settled in Asheville, North Carolina, and decided to extend similar standards of comfort and hospitable service to other world wanderers.

They purchased a 1904 stone and shingle house in near ruins, and embarked on a five-year restoration project to bring the structure back to its original beauty. Decorated with art and furnishings collected during years of travel, the North Lodge on Oakland Bed & Breakfast is an inviting and comfortable stop on any traveler's itinerary.

For information, call 1-800-282-3602 or visit their web site at www.northlodge.com.

THE BILTMORE ESTATE

Ｇeorge Washington Vanderbilt was only ten years old when he made his first transatlantic voyage, tagging along for years to come on trips overseas with his family. Sometimes, he would accompany his mother and sister on shopping excursions. At other times, he would venture with his father, an avid art collector. As the young George Vanderbilt began to mature, so did his own penchant for seeing the world and he traveled far beyond the familiar Paris boulevards and London streets to explore the exotic realms of Egypt, India, and the Far East.

Yet, when it came to building a family home for his vast collection of arts and antiques, many purchased during his travels, he chose to settle in Asheville, North Carolina. The young Vanderbilt called on architect Richard Morris Hunt and landscape architect Frederick Law Olmsted to create Biltmore House, America's largest private home, and the estate that surrounds it. Today, the 250-room French Renaissance chateau and National Historic Landmark has become a popular destination for modern-day travelers.

Still owned and operated by Vanderbilt's heirs, Biltmore House reflects the passions of a citizen of the world. On view in the stately home, its architecture inspired by French chateaux of the Loire Valley, is Vanderbilt's collection of more

than 70,000 priceless objects. In the Banquet Hall hang five 16th century Flemish tapestries. In the Library is an 18th century Antonio Pelligrini ceiling painting, *The Chariot of Aurora*, from the Palazzo Pisani in Italy. And throughout are delicate porcelain figures, bronzes, and ceramics that Vanderbilt discovered during his 1892 trip to Japan.

Surrounding the home are 75 acres of gardens and grounds that reveal many horticultural influences from 19th century France, England, and America. Spectacular vistas from the English Walled Garden or the Italian Renaissance pools evoke Vanderbilt's love for the Blue Ridge Mountains he called home. Today, Biltmore's doors are open year-round to travelers from around the world.

George Vanderbilt (seated at left) on voyage in 1890. For more information on the Biltmore Estate, call 1-800-543-2961 or visit Biltmore's web site at www.biltmore.com.

ALL ABOARD

There's nothing quite like the thrill of an upcoming trip. After the schedule is set and the reservations are booked, you can begin dreaming about exciting sights, sounds, smells, and tastes in exotic faraway places. But the daydreaming about new adventures fades quickly once you begin thinking of all that must get done before you leave. That's when the Big Question rears its ugly head: "What am I going to wear?"

Whether you're planning a serious business trip, across-the-country cycling marathon, or a leisurely sightseeing trek, the clothes you will take become very important. In fact, your travel wardrobe starts to occupy your thoughts a lot. You agonize over the perfect outfit for each occasion and location, hoping that you can cram every perfect item into one bag. You search your closet, sewing pattern stash, and the department store racks or mail order catalogs for that key garment that will wear well,

keep you warm or cool as needed, and be appropriate for meeting the Queen or tracking wildlife. You're not looking for ordinary run-of-the-mill clothing. You need hard-working, versatile, interchangeable items that will carry you around the world.

For years, fashion designers have recognized the need for efficient and stylish travel clothing. American designer Claire McCardell, noted for her attention to practicality, showed a six-piece wardrobe of interchangeable separates in the mid-1930s. This travel ensemble of skirt, jacket, slacks, shorts, and tops was meant to provide the active wayfarer with

an easy-to-mix selection of good-looking outfits. However, the fashionable travelers of the day were not ready for McCardell's forward-thinking designs.

In 1948, designer Vera Maxwell's travel ensemble of tweed jacket, slacks, and silk print blouse coincided with the increase in airline usage. As more women hopped on planes, they demanded practical clothing to travel with them. Maxwell even added a novel touch: plastic-lined pockets to hold toothbrush, washcloth, or other essentials.

In the 1960s, designer and globetrotter Bonnie Cashin presented travel wardrobes composed of layered separates for the busy, modern woman. She even incorporated "security" purses into her designs. Cashin's acknowledgment of a woman's desire to look stylish when tripping around the world or across town earned her a 1963 award from Sports Illustrated for being "the master equipper of all travelers."

In 1997, designer Isabel Toledo introduced her "packing" skirt, a two-panel linen fashion, whose panels ingeniously fold flat into a circle for easy stowing in a small suitcase.

And in 1999, the adventurous designer Norma Kamali created a poly-jersey over-the-shoulder travel bag, so the wearer could stash her coordinating poly-jersey separates and hit the road at a moment's notice.

The challenge of packing an entire trip's worth of clothing into carry-on luggage has motivated travelers of all sorts to develop good ideas for garment design and inventive approaches to dressing well day after day, without resorting to an all-khaki collection of utilitarian tourist clothes. You, too, can master cosmopolitan style and on-the-road efficiency, yet still express your individual cachet.

So get comfortable, buckle your seatbelt, and browse the following pages. You will see seven coordinated wardrobes by sewing designers like you that were created to satisfy specific travel conditions. You also will find guidelines for planning and creating the perfect wardrobe for you, ingenious sewing projects to make every trip a breeze, and handy survival tips from seasoned travelers. Happy sewing—and Bon Voyage!

It's exhilarating to travel to a new place, where you will be surrounded by strangers. You are free to create any impression you desire, be anyone you want to be, dress in any fashion you choose. You don't have to be another khaki-clad tourist who resembles every other globe-trotter. Whether you're planning a trip abroad or a weekend jaunt to a nearby city, you are free to make a conscious decision about the wardrobe you will wear.

Take advantage of this ability to choose. Consider whether you want to look absolutely in step with the fashion trends of the moment, dress like the locals, project the image of a traveling professional, blend in with the other tourists, or proudly stand out as the creative individual you are. Once you decide which traveling persona you wish to be, it's easier to plan your mobile wardrobe.

Because you are creatively inclined and like to sew, you most likely enjoy expressing yourself with the clothes you wear, at home and elsewhere. When you travel, you won't want to take an entire suitcase of those neutral, go-with-anything "basics," leaving all your favorite interesting garments in your closet. You will want to express your personal style and show off the beautiful fashions you have made.

However, many of your extra special one-of-a-kind originals may not be very versatile. They may go with one or two other garments and that's about it. They may not even be very practical, but they are fun to wear and you are proud to showcase your creative talents.

All the travel books wisely tell you to plan the most interchangeable travel wardrobe possible. You may have heard the expression, "same clothes, different outfits." You are urged to strive for flexibility by choosing a selection of versatile components that mix and match with each other in as many ways as possible. The goal is to achieve the maximum number of outfit possibilities without packing your entire closet or having to tote huge steamer trunks full of clothes.

Besides, lots of luggage ties you down. You want to be noticed for your interesting, unique, and creative clothes, yet you also want to be a liberated traveler—able to dash on and off trains and planes, with the smallest and lightest bags possible. Free to get out and see the world, leaving throngs of travelers behind waiting for their luggage.

You don't have to give up your creative fashion sense for mobility. In fact, an upcoming trip is the perfect opportunity to sew some new originals that will also be good traveling companions. Careful planning combined with ingenious sewing can help you take your personal style around the world and make the on-the-road impression you desire.

Every trip is different and will require a different combination of outfits. Your needs for an antique-buying jaunt to London will be different than an adventure travel experience in Africa. A craft tour through Scandinavia will differ from the same type of tour through Asia. There is no single wardrobe configuration that will meet every need, so don't get caught up in devising THE perfect travel wardrobe. What is perfect for one trip will be uncomfortable or inappropriate for another.

Instead, well before your departure date, study the different features of your upcoming trip. Pick your itinerary apart into single days or segments of days, and analyze what each segment will require. As you assemble the components of your travel wardrobe, you can ensure that there will be something perfect to wear for each moment of each day. You need to start this analysis early, to be sure you'll have enough time to sew, shop, or mail order key components that are not already in your closet or dresser. Besides, it's fun to think ahead to the places you'll see and the experiences you'll have.

You'll get your enthusiasm fired up and ready to go.

If you are a spur-of-the-moment traveler, who takes advantage of super cut rates by giving up advance scheduling, planning is still very important. If you get a confirmed reservation for a trip leaving the next day, you won't want to stay up all night rummaging through closet and drawers, trying to piece together an adequate wardrobe. As you throw things into your carry-on, you will probably wonder which item you're forgetting that you'll absolutely need three days hence, when you're thousands of miles from home. At the same time, you'll pack several "just-in-case-I-need-it" items that add weight to your bags and never get worn. Therefore, it's important to get organized even when you're not packing for a specific trip.

If you're a traveler at heart, you should ALWAYS be ready to leave at a moment's notice. In this case, put together a core wardrobe of dependable items that have worked well in most travel conditions. You might even want to keep these items separated from your everyday clothing, so they'll be easy to grab and pack. Alternatively, make a checklist of items that have passed the travel wardrobe test so you can refer to it and quickly pack your bags when you get that phone call offering a flight the next morning. Once you know the core wardrobe is taken care of, you can add or subtract particular items based on your current destination.

WHAT ARE THE FEATURES OF YOUR TRIP?

Even the shortest trip can be analyzed according to different features, including destination, length of stay, method of travel, and weather. You must consider all of these factors so you can pull together the most appropriate wardrobe possible and not wonder what you're going to wear after the second day. By knowing the various requirements of your itinerary and making a wardrobe plan, you can be perfectly dressed and free to enjoy instead of agonizing over how you look.

TYPE OF TRIP

Is this jaunt a vacation, business trip, family obligation, or a combination? If you're going to a tropical resort for a much-needed vacation, you won't need to sew or purchase a new raincoat. You can be casual, pack the brightest of colors, and probably don't have to worry about appropriate dress codes. If you are making a business trip that will include lots of meetings, you may need to dress conservatively, take account of local attitudes about professional dress, and plan for lots of time in chilly air-conditioned offices. If your trip is a mixed bag that includes a job interview, family reunion, and some sightseeing, you'll be packing some

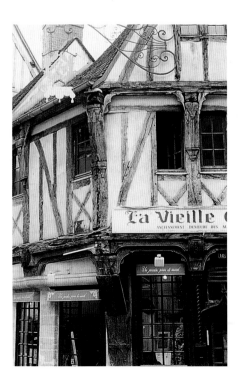

double-duty clothes along with a few special event outfits. The assortment will be different than if your combination trip includes a trade show, some business calls, and a few evenings of theater.

It can be helpful to draw out a trip chart or calendar that lists every day you will be gone and its various "event" segments. Morning, afternoon, and evening categories are logical breakdowns for each day, but your particular trip may require additional time segments. For example, many professional conferences schedule meetings or seminars in the morning and early afternoon, leaving "Free Time" from 4:00-6:00 p.m. The evenings may then be divided into various time slots for a keynote address or dinner/reception, followed by a more casual networking event for conferees. You may want to change clothes after the seminars for your free-time sightseeing or exercise; then, you'll change again for dinner, and perhaps once more for casual club-hopping with fellow professionals.

If you have analyzed your entire travel plan by the types of appearances

you must make, you'll have a good start toward building adequate wardrobe coverage from dawn until dark. This trip chart can be useful in many different ways, before you leave home and while you're on the

BUYING FABRIC ABROAD?

If you love to sew, then fabric-shopping is probably one of the great pleasures of traveling. There's nothing like the thrill of finding antique lace in Brussels, masterful ikat in Bali, or a brilliantly colored print in Senegal. To be sure you bring enough home for your next project, refer to these metric conversions.

⅛" = 3.2 mm	⅛ yd = .15 m
¼" = 6.4 mm	¼ yd = .25 m
⅜" = 1 cm	⅜ yd = .35 m
½" = 1.25 cm	½ yd = .5 m
⅝" = 1.6 cm	⅝ yd = .6 m
¾" = 2 cm	¾ yd = .7 m
1" = 2.5 cm	1 yd = .95 m
45" = 115 cm/1.1 m	1½ yds = 1.4 m
54" = 137 cm/1.4 m	2 yds = 1.85 m
60" = 152 cm/1.5 m	3 yds = 2.75m

road. Use it as a planning tool when you're evaluating how to fill gaps in your wardrobe, as a checklist when packing your bags, and as a reference when getting dressed for the various events of each day or for reviewing your outfit possibilities halfway through the trip. It can even be helpful if you're tempted to make purchases, because it will remind you of the various functions you still have to attend and, therefore, which items in the street bazaar or boulevard boutique might be perfect acquisitions.

WHERE AND WHEN ARE YOU GOING?

What you take with you will be influenced as much by where you're going as what you'll be doing. A January business trip to Chicago will have very different requirements than a September conference in San

Antonio, even if each day's events will be similar. Weather will be an important consideration when getting ready to go, particularly if you will be visiting more than one place and the weather conditions are different in each. Refer to a travel guide, almanac, or the televised weather channels to get an idea of the average temperatures for the

time of year you'll be going, so you will be prepared without having to over-pack. If your trip will include fluctuating weather conditions, you'll have a good reason to make that lightweight fleece vest you've been wanting, or to experiment with a sun hat or sarong.

Will special events be happening at your destination during your stay? Spoleto in Charleston? The running of the bulls in Pamplona? Cinco de Mayo in Mexico City? Mardi Gras in New Orleans? Bastille Day in Paris? If you know about any scheduled events ahead of time, you can be sure to carry suitable attire.

Are there customs and cultural mores you must consider that might influence your selection of garments? Any good travel guide can alert you to respectful dress guidelines for travel in many destinations, from touring cathedrals in Italy to shopping at Middle Eastern bazaars. By knowing about local dress codes

in advance, you will be better prepared and you won't risk offending people or being turned away from sightseeing stops.

HOW WILL YOU BE TRAVELING AND HOW LONG WILL IT TAKE?

The method of travel is an important consideration in choosing a travel-friendly wardrobe, and determining how much you can pack. You will want to be comfortable en route to your destination, so you don't get tired and irritable before you even arrive. If you will be on trains and planes for long periods of time, plan ahead by choosing travel outfits that are comfy and that still look good when you disembark. Think about how much time you'll spend traveling compared to the time you'll spend exploring your destination. The proportion of "getting-there"

*T*ake two yards (1.85 m) each of fabric and cord with you. The fabric packs flat and can fulfill so many needs—a sarong, carrying cloth, sheet, bed covering, shawl, towel, head wrap, or sun shade. Put the fabric on the cord for a shower curtain, if privacy is needed. And use the cord as a clothesline, belt, or to tie luggage securely closed. When you're ready to come home, leave the fabric behind or trade it in for a new two-yard (1.85-m) length.

KATHY TRIPLETT,
artist

clothes to "being-there" clothes will vary greatly from trip to trip. Again, planning ahead will make sure you're comfortable and well-dressed on every day of the trip.

WHAT AMENITIES ARE AVAILABLE AT YOUR DESTINATION?

The contents of your luggage may also change depending on what's available once you get where you're going. Consider, in advance, whether you'll have access to laundry or dry cleaning services, whether there will be ample storage for clothing, or whether you'll even have protection from the weather. Will you be right in the middle of a shopping mecca? If so, you may not want to take as much so you'll feel free to make some new purchases. Will you be traveling the countryside, far from civilization? If so, you'll need to prepare for every wardrobe contingency. Will you be staying put for an extended period, in a room with ample storage space? If so, you can take everything you need. Will you be spending lots of time in air-conditioned, unheated, or brutally sunny locations? Make sure you're well-prepared for optimum comfort. If conditions turn out to be extreme, you will have to make a local shopping trip, to stock up on what you need.

Once you've got a good idea of your overall trip and what it will require, you're ready to start getting specific about what to take. Whether you're buying or sewing new travel clothing, or making do with what you've already got, take a "less is more" approach to building a travel wardrobe. Start with your trip chart that details the types of functions you'll need to dress for and the characteristics of the places you're going. Then, choose a basic core wardrobe plan that meets the various conditions of your particular trip.

BUILD ON A FOUNDATION

What is a basic core wardrobe? It's, quite simply, a skeleton selection of component garments that are comfortable to wear and fit you well, and appropriate for the type of trip, locations you'll be visiting, and amount of time you'll be away from home. Core garments should also mix and match with each other in several different ways, as well as with your supplementary or accent items, those garments that you add on to the core wardrobe to make it uniquely you.

Core pieces include jacket, skirt, slacks, and top. For example, a black suit and slacks with a white top can give you several different outfits,

especially when adding other complementary garments, such as red sweater, black and white print blouse, black T-shirt, and several patterned scarves. You continue to build on to the basic black/white core grouping to arrive at a selection of outfits that will be easy to carry and perfect for the different occasions of your trip. If you're visiting a cold, rainy corner of the world, a microfiber raincoat with button in lining might be part of your core group; on the other hand, if you're trekking through the American West, several pairs of walking shorts with coordinating T-shirts will be centrally

important. But as long as you start with a flexible skeleton grouping, it will be easy to add on supplementary items to result in a wardrobe that is perfectly customized to your individual travel needs.

If you don't know where to begin identifying basic wardrobe items, look through the several travel-related mail order catalogs that are available. A quick scan of many lifestyle and travel magazines will reveal these catalog offerings, along with 1-800 numbers that make it easy to get in touch. These and other companies, including luggage and travel/touring stores in your community, specialize in efficient wardrobe planning and packing. As you consider all the available options, from conservative two-piece suits to casual walking slacks and camp shirts, you'll quickly notice the type of "look" that appeals to your personal sense of style. That look may be feminine, business-like, ethnic, or rustic country. Look at how companion garments are put together with the various core styles, to provide a whole array of wearing options.

Make a visit to your own closet or sewing pattern collection and begin selecting the core garments that feel the most appropriate for you and your trip. If you've already got a great selection of jackets and skirts you've sewn over the years, choose one of each as a starting point. Then, look further for complementary tops and bottoms that dovetail perfectly with the original skirt/jacket combo. If you identify a "missing" item that would be nice to take along, such as a shirt-type jacket that can also be worn over another top to provide a little extra warmth, you can choose a favorite pattern and make it out of beautiful fabric that coordinates with the core group, and have it ready for your departure.

CHOOSE HARD-WORKING COLORS

When it comes to colors, remember the "less is more" philosophy. The fewer colors you carry along, the more likely everything will go together. This doesn't mean you have to leave a favorite piece home just because it's a wildly different color; if you know from your trip chart that you've got a special event coming

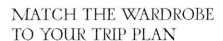

If you must attend an important event as soon as you get to your destination, consider carrying some kind of easy-to-pack outfit like a broomstick skirt or other item that will survive a cramped carry-on tote. Then, if you suffer delayed or lost luggage, you will still have something nice to change into.

CARYNE FINLAY,
artist

up and you have room to carry it in your suitcase, by all means take it along. You'll feel great when you wear it, and you'll look excitingly different than the other travelers. However, try to stick mainly to basics that you won't tire of, that wear well, and are low-maintenance. The most popular colors for travel wear are black, navy, and dark neutrals like brown, tan, and khaki. They are popular because they successfully mix with each other, and with other basics like white, ivory, and beige. Add spots of accent color to your basic palette with jewelry, belts, vests, and the ever-versatile scarf.

For the most practical travel, stick with solid colors or very subtle patterns. Again, you want as many different combinations from your selection of individual components as possible. A trip away from home is not the time or place to try and put together plaids, tweeds, and stripes in pleasing ways. Every minute spent in front of the hotel mirror, problem-solving your outfit for the day, is a minute you could be out exploring the world. Dark and solid colors are good at transitioning from day to evening occasions, and for disguising dirt or stains. However, a subtle tweed will work well for one piece in your core group, especially a jacket or slacks. Even though it's not a solid, this type of fabric will still coordinate successfully with other colors and patterns, and will very successfully appear clean and neat for the entire trip.

MATCH THE WARDROBE TO YOUR TRIP PLAN

Be sure that your core wardrobe matches well with the trip you're taking. The Broadway Boogie wardrobe on page 52 was designed for a precisely focused trip—a week of dinner and theater dates in New

York City. The individual pieces are dressier than for a sight-seeing wardrobe and they all interchange with each other in attractive ways. Additionally, the designer made sure they are comfortable to wear and accommodating of slight figure changes during a week of good eating and lots of sitting. For an on-foot sightseeing trip, the Fall Wardrobe on page 48 features just as much flexibility but is geared toward more casual looks and several options for layering, an important consideration when visiting inside and outside points of interest. This wardrobe also builds in a couple of options for the dressier occasion, such as a nice dinner out or museum opening, as well as some original garments and hand-crafted jewelry to showcase the designer's creative talents.

If you're not sure you'll have everything you'll need, lay out all the components on your bed and then arrange them in various combinations. Somehow, it's easier to visualize when moving actual garments around than thinking about the possibilities in your head. Look at each individual item with a critical eye. Can it be worn with at least one other item, and preferably with two or more? Do you have combinations for every day of your trip? Refer to your trip chart, to jog your memory about all the occasions and locations on your itinerary. You can even

expand the chart to write in the outfits you've put together for each event. Then you won't even have to think about getting dressed each day, because you will have marked it down ahead of time.

As long as everything is still on your bed, it's easy to arrange and rearrange. When you've got the core wardrobe staked out, start enhancing the various outfits with your special one-of-a-kind garments, such as a unique applique vest or pieced jacket. Get out all your scarves and see how many different ways you can mix them with the core wardrobe, to extend outfit possibilities even more. Pull in your fabric

stash or swatches from the sewing room to see if there are perfect complements; if so, look through your patterns to identify the best garment and get started sewing as soon as possible.

Try to complete this wardrobe assessment and layout as far in advance of your departure as possible. If you determine that the perfect missing piece needs to be sewn, you'll have time to complete it and make it special. While it will be nice to have this unique garment with you on the trip, it will be even better if you have enough time to do a good job. Plus, you will get the benefit of its special qualities when you return home and can include it in your everyday wardrobe.

The velvety skirts, dresses, and tops made with a touch of Spandex are perfect for traveling. There's no wrinkling. Just give them a good shake and they're ready to wear.

JOAN BAEZ,
musician and entertainer

If you're going to sew some new fashions to take with you, there are style considerations to keep in mind when scanning the pattern books or looking through your own supply of sewing patterns. These characteristics will make it easier to pack the resulting garments into limited luggage space and will enhance their on-the-road wearability.

You will probably gravitate toward a loose and layered style for most of your travel ensembles, so choose patterns that feature simple, uncluttered construction and uncomplicated styling. The more stripped down and basic the garment, the easier it will interchange with other travel wardrobe items, giving you the results you want—many different outfits from the same clothes. Additionally, the simplest styles will require the least care while away from home. You won't need to carry a travel iron to press intricate seams or tailored construction.

For example, a simple A-line skirt and classic button-front blouse will mix and match with any number of jackets, sweaters, and slacks, plus

they will fold easily and pack flat. This saves room in your suitcase for other items or exotic new purchases, and saves time figuring out what to wear each day because they are versatile, easy-to-wear garments. A simple, collarless box jacket will pack easier than a classic tailored style that may require stuffing the collar with tissue to maintain its shape. It also will fit over light sweaters easier than a fitted jacket, thus giving you more options for layering and weather protection. It is

casual by itself, but can also be dressed up with a classy scarf, pretty shawl, or glittering brooch.

Straight, jewel-neck chemise-type dresses are sleek and sophisticated when worn alone, but they also look classy belted, or worn with a scarf around the shoulders or hips, under a jacket or sweater, or as a tunic over leggings. A fussy dress with full gathered skirt and lots of frilly details doesn't layer with other garments very comfortably, and it's difficult to combine it with other items for a changing array of looks. So stick with the simplest styles that you can dress up, down, or differently with other companion garments.

Stay away from too much surface texture, such as ruffles, tucks, pleats, and other three-dimensional effects. Clothes with these features may be interesting, but they require more maintenance and they take up extra space in your luggage. Don't waste a fraction of packing space on bulky surface treatments you don't need. Instead, if you seek embellishment, look for patterns that feature color blocking or pieced construction, or spiff up the finished item with some embroidery, beadwork, or other flat decorative effect. Even better, rely on an interesting selection of accessories to make the same basic garment look different each time you wear it.

EVALUATE CONSTRUCTION FOR ON-THE-ROAD COMFORT

Watch out for construction methods that will interfere with comfortable wear, especially if you plan to layer wardrobe components in different combinations, depending on the occasion or the weather. Think of your layers from the inside out, and be sure the outer layers will fit easily over the inner layers. Be especially attentive to neckline and sleeve construction methods that guarantee easy layering and complementary wearing. For example, if you make a roomy box-style jacket with set-in sleeves, don't make a dolman-sleeve dress to wear underneath it. It won't be comfortable to wear the set-in sleeves over the loose dolman style, and it won't look good either. By the same token, a classic tailored jacket won't fit well over a roomy quilted vest and a jewel-neck pullover tunic won't fit well over a loose cowl-neck blouse.

Don't forget to evaluate how the various hem lengths of your wardrobe components relate to one another, especially in all their mix-and-match combinations. A very slight difference in hem lengths between a tunic shirt and a jacket will appear as if you made a measurement error; increase the difference for greater contrast between the two hemlines and the result will appear as a conscious design decision.

Your choice of garment design and construction features is important to wearing comfort, as well as appearance. It's difficult to tolerate tightly fitting armholes, too-fitted waistlines, and too-small necklines when you must wear them for hours at a time and in situations where you cannot move around much, as on airplanes or in waiting rooms. You'll also be eating more and exercising less, and if you happen to put on a little weight, your clothes will still need to fit comfortably and with enough wearing ease. If you will be walking or sitting for extended periods of time, or if you find yourself having to run to make a travel connection, be sure that you won't be hampered by your clothing.

Choose styles with enough ease to accommodate or fit over any security features you wish to incorporate in the sewing, such as hidden pockets and security wallets. You will defeat the purpose of a hidden money belt if your garments aren't loose enough to comfortably slide over it. Or you will have to lug around separate carryalls if your garments don't have enough ease to include inner pockets or around-the-neck passport totes. Too-fitted garments will look stuffed if you try to incorporate such secret compartments in them and they won't be comfortable to wear. If you plan to camouflage security features in your travel wardrobe, be sure the garment designs are loose-fitting enough that you will appreciate the effort you made to include them.

Before you start cutting and stitching, visualize how each garment will pack. Look for straight seams and uncomplicated silhouettes that will roll up compactly or fold easily, without disturbing the shape of the garment too much. If you don't want to limit your travel skirts to straight or A-line styles, sew a pattern for a gathered waist style and make it out of a crinkly fabric. Then you can scrunch the finished skirt up from waist to hem and tie the whole garment in an overhand knot; the scrunching and tying preserves the intended look of this never-iron garment and you can stuff the knotted skirt into small nooks and crannies of your luggage.

GET THE MOST OUT OF YOUR PATTERNS

Look for ways to transform basic patterns to make the finished garments more flexible, whether you sew them as reversibles or make some of the parts detachable. Reversible garments are an obvious and efficient way to increase wardrobe options without increasing the number of components. And you can create two different looks with one garment, whether dressy on one side and casual on the other, or solid color on one side and patterned on the other. Almost any sewing pattern can be adjusted so it can be worn on either side, and the resulting two-in-one garment will actually multiply out to many outfits when combined with other reversible items. The Broadway Boogie Wardrobe on page 52, with its four-way reversible tunic and coordinating reversible jacket and pants, is an entire closet-full of outfits in just a handful of garments. With a reversible item, you don't even have to change the main components of an outfit; simply turn a vest or jacket inside out and you're ready to go out to dinner after a day of touring. Scarves can be reversible, too, further multiplying the color and style results of various outfits. See page 22 for tips about sewing reversibles successfully and page 37 about different ways to tie scarves.

Fashions with detachable features require a bit more planning and construction ingenuity than simple reversibles, but the results can be worth it. The Sungold raincoat with button-in lining on page 38 is a practical and beautiful example of detachable design. The coat without lining is perfect for warmer weather, layering over the three-piece suit, and can also do double duty as a bathrobe. Button in the lining and the traveler can weather more dramatic climates or location changes without sacrificing any style. The vest with detachable and reversible capelets on page 79 is a truly cre-

ative approach to designing a versatile fashion that can be worn in many different ways. The roomy armholes of the vest make it easy to wear over sweaters or other warm tops, eliminating the need for carrying a coat. The capelets can be swapped or removed altogether for different looks. Detachable collars are another quick and easy way to multiply the same outfit's looks, and they save the time of sewing entire garments. They also offer the opportunity of experimenting with new techniques in a small area, to let your creativity shine.

If you choose simple, basic styles for your wardrobe components, you will find it easier to innovate their wearing options. It's easier to sew reversible styles or detachable features when the garment design is streamlined and uncomplicated. Plus, it's so much easier to accessorize uncluttered garments because the scarf, jewelry, sash, or other "extra" won't have to compete with pockets, ruffles, or fancy details. Additionally, you can more easily add a creative touch or accent to a basic style than to one that is already full of design features. Your original applique design will take center stage on a basic jacket instead of competing with the built-in features of a more complicated style. If you piece or hand weave custom fabric, let the beautiful yardage shine in a simple design that doesn't cut up the fabric into lots of small areas.

A WORD ABOUT RESPECTFUL DRESS

Consider the cultural norms of the countries you will be visiting and keep them in mind when you're searching for patterns. Local customs may influence your choice of sleeves (long, short, or sleeveless), hem length, and overall garment fit. With a little advance research, you can avoid embarrassment later on or the chance of being turned away from sightseeing locations because of inappropriate dress.

You might want to avoid wearing a lot of certain colors, depending on where you travel. For example, white is considered funereal in China and is the color of death in Mexico, whereas solid black is a funereal color in Thailand and Japan. In Brazil, green and yellow are the national colors, so don't wear them together.

Other general guidelines that are universal include no short skirts, bare shoulders, or blue jeans. Most locales are more conservative than the cosmopolitan big cities, so wear your skirts longer and full enough that you can sit on the floor comfortably, especially in countries where seating is low to the ground. Always carry a shawl or large scarf that you can use to cover your head and/or shoulders before entering places of worship. And, while jeans are acceptable garb in some Westernized areas, why take them along? Denim is bulky to pack, takes forever to dry, and looks too casual for most places.

In short, a slightly more dressed-up approach to your travel wardrobe will ensure that you encounter open doors and welcoming hosts instead of being dismissed as another disrespectful tourist.

I'm on the road for months at a time, and these are some of the traveling tips that never fail me. Don't pack your jewelry in checked baggage; instead, make sure it's in your purse or carry-on. Don't pack a lot of color schemes, because then you have to carry too many hard-to-pack shoes. Instead, limit garment colors and pack more hose; hosiery doesn't take much room and it can change the look of an outfit. Carry one pair of shoulder pads that can attach to every garment with hook-and-loop tape. And don't forget to take your vitamins; I take high-stress multiple vitamins and never get sick on the road.

SANDRA BETZINA,
sewing expert, author, and television personality

TECHNICAL TIPS FOR TWO-SIDED FASHIONS

When you're traveling, reversibles can more than double the outfit possibilities of your wardrobe to give you plenty of mix-and-match options for every occasion. Almost any garment can be made in a reversible version, but some styles work better than others. These guidelines will help you turn every reversible garment into a double-duty fashion.

▶ Choose basic, simple pattern styles that are not cluttered with multiple elements and tailored construction details. It will be easier to sew such styles in double layers and you won't have the added bulk of numerous seams, pleats, and complicated tailoring.

▶ Select fabrics that won't show through to the other side, unless you want them to do so for a desired effect. Make sure both layers are compatible in weight, drape, and method of cleaning. If one side is sturdy cotton and the other is drapey rayon, the garment will never hang right as a reversible. And you won't want a two-layer garment that requires dry cleaning on one side and machine washing on the other.

▶ Choose a thread color that coordinates with both layers, or else thread the top to match one layer and the bobbin to match the other.

In this case, take care that you keep the bobbin-matching fabric on the bottom while you sew. Another option is to use clear thread,

although this can be hard to work with if you sew in the evening hours.

▶ To allow enough space for two layers of fabric, you may have to cut the pattern one size larger. If the garment style is roomy, just cut the more fitted areas one size larger, such as shoulders and armholes.

▶ Because you don't stitch a traditional hem in a reversible garment, cut hem allowances down to seam

allowance widths. You'll save a bit of fabric and won't have to trim away the excess after stitching the two-layered seams at the bottom of the garment and sleeves.

▶ If you're making a reversible version of a skirt with kick pleat, change the pleat to a straight slit and move it to a side seam, where it can be easily turned from one side to the other.

▶ Be sure to leave an opening that's big enough to turn the garment out to the right side, and position openings in discreet locations, such as back hem or side seams. See the Four Seasons Vests on page 72 and Have Vest Will Travel on page 76 for different approaches to stitching and turning reversible garments.

▶ Substitute button loop closures for standard buttonholes, so the garment can be buttoned from either side. You can sew buttons on both sides or just on one side. If you choose the one-side method, the loops can still reach the buttons inside the garment.

▶ Press darts in the two layers in opposite directions, so they don't pile up on top of one another and add bulk to the finished garment.

▶ To keep one layer from rolling over and peeking out from the wrong side, edgestitch the garment all around. Additionally, hand- or machine-tack the two layers together at seam intersections and underarms to keep the layers from shifting and to ensure that the garment settles into the correct position after turning.

▶ If you don't want to edgestitch a reversible garment, consider piping the seams. The piping hides any little bit of reverse side peeking out, especially on garments made from drapey fabrics. Plus, it adds a nice finishing touch. See the Four-Way Reversible Tunic in the Broadway Boogie Wardrobe on page 52.

▶ To eliminate the bulk of doubled-up seams, stitch the two layers with wrong sides together and then bind the raw edges with decorative seam binding, custom-made bias binding that coordinates perfectly with the fabric, or other braid or trim.

▶ When considering embellishments and other artful additions to your reversible garment, try to determine ahead of time how much bulk or thickness will be added to the garment and how such decorations may affect comfort. You won't want a scratchy thread decoration next to your skin when you turn the embellished layer to the inside. Instead, choose flat or low-texture appliqué treatments or make all your decorative effects detachable—you can simply take them off and even wear them as creative accessories with other garments.

*P*rotect your passport by making a duplicate and carrying it in a different place than the real one. Have an extra set of photos made, photocopy the information page, photocopy your birth certificate, make pencil rubbings of any seals, and include a list of important contacts and phone numbers. You may also want to photocopy your credit cards and other forms of identification.

CECILY FIRESTEIN,
antique jewelry dealer

*M*y Sandra Betzina Coat pattern is perfect for traveling. It's clean-finished, with French seams on the outside and the deep dolman sleeves make it easy to layer the coat over other clothes. Sew it in wool melton for a classy, warm coat, then make it again as a raincoat in crinkle nylon or microfiber and wear it over the melton. Just cut the raincoat ½" (1.25 cm) longer.

SANDRA BETZINA,
sewing expert, author, and television personality

*I*f you travel on business and must carry a lot of files or papers, transport them in a wheeled suitcase instead of overloading your briefcase. You might even be able to fit all your clothes in the same bag.

CHARLOTTE LUNSFORD BERRY,
professional volunteer and seasoned traveler

*A*lways line your travel skirts. Then you don't have to pack slips and worry about them being the right length. Lined garments also resist wrinkles better than unlined. If one of your skirts is a wrap style, use a straight skirt pattern for the lining; when the wind blows the wrapped front open, your modesty will be preserved.

MARY PARKER,
designer

Before heading to your favorite sewing store to shop for travel fabrics, take a look in your closet. You can immediately identify the garments that are most comfortable to wear, that are warm or cool, and that are easy-care. Pull these items out and consider why they are so successful. Is it the loose fit, simple construction, or elastic waist? Or is it the wonderfully soft, lightweight, washable fabric? Use these comfort qualities to help you select both the styles and fabrics for your travel wardrobe.

When browsing the fabric store with your comfort qualities in mind, feel free to follow your heart to a particular bolt, but use your head before spending any money. Apply a critical eye, and hand, to evaluate any fabric's on-the-road worthiness. You will naturally expect your travel fabrics to look good mile after mile, but you also want them to be comfortable, wrinkle-resistant, lightweight, and easy to care for. These conditions narrow the selection to some basic fabrics that you probably already love to sew with.

CLASSIC COMFORT

Knits, crepes, jerseys, and other soft, pliable fabrics are good choices for travel clothes because they drape well, are soft and comfy to wear, and they don't wrinkle as easily as crisply woven materials. Think of yourself sitting in a cramped airplane, auto, or bus seat for hours and you'll decide that you'd rather be wearing a cozy wool jersey than a bulky corduroy. In a warm season or climate, you'll certainly choose a breathable natural fiber or blend over polyester. And if you're heading to the cold country, you'll prefer lightweight insulating layers to a bulky overcoat.

Silks, tropical weight wools, wool jersey and crepe, some rayons, and cotton blends are often used for travel garments. These are the natural fabrics you will see in the travel clothing catalogs. They are comfortable, lightweight, breathable, and they still drape well after enduring hours or days of wear. They are resilient and spring back into shape after being folded, crumpled, or forced to sit for hours in a cramped seat. This springy quality is built into the fabric structure in knits, crepes, and jerseys, and is inherent in the individual fibers of a wool fabric. Lightweight cotton, especially gauze, is great for hot climates because it is lightweight and very cool. It's also a good choice for an intentionally crinkled look, so use it for casual garments.

Handwoven fabrics lend themselves well to travel gear, because they drape easily and are wrinkle-resistant. The subtle and interesting colorations of many handwovens, created by different colors in the warp and weft, coordinate beautifully with other fabrics. And the unique handcrafted quality makes them extra special garments that can do double duty as daywear and dressy evening wear. See "Handwovens Make Good Traveling Companions" on page 29 for more about this creative cloth.

ON THE CUTTING EDGE

Many new high-tech fabrics and fabric treatments have been developed in recent years that help you stay comfortable no matter where your voyage takes you or what time of year. These fabrics have been a mainstay of the sport clothing revolution of the past two decades. You see them in clothing and equipment for running, hiking, bicycling, camping, rock climbing, skiing, swimming, and other activities. Stretch fabrics, water repellent materials, insulating fibers, and "breathable" cloth help you stay cool and collected, or warm and dry.

Many of the fabrics used for parkas, ski pants, and rainwear are now available by the yard. This vastly increases the options you have for everyday sewing as well as travel wardrobe planning. Your local fabric shop probably has a growing selection of outerwear fabrics, microfiber, and stretch fibers. Take advantage of these new discoveries to achieve an on-the-road wardrobe of custom originals that are also truly comfortable to wear.

Use your mail order catalogs of outdoor clothing and camping gear to familiarize yourself with the trademarked names of fabrics and their benefits. You'll see Coolmax®, Supplex®, Gore-Tex®, Velcro®, Polartec®, Lycra®, Teflon®,

Cordura®, Tencel®, and others, by themselves or blended with other fibers. These revolutionary fabrics were designed for particular purposes governed by the demands of certain activities and environments. Although you may not be dog-sledding across the Arctic or doing research in the rain forest, you can benefit from the features of these manmade fabric wonders.

If you will be hiking, biking, or otherwise working up a sweat, you'll be interested in the fabrics that help wick perspiration away from the body, so you will stay dry and comfortable in warm or cold weather.

Synthetic coatings and surface treatments render some fabrics completely water-repellent or simply moisture-resistant, convenient in damp or downright wet locations. Other high-tech fabrics are easy to wash, quick-drying, particularly breathable, or especially resistant to wind.

Depending on where you're going and what you're planning to wear, look for the features and fabrics that will be most appropriate. Ask the sales staff at the fabric store for guidance about the particular characteristics of the high-tech fabrics they carry and any special sewing techniques required. See "New-Tech Fabrics For The Globetrotter" on page 27 for more information about these and other materials.

COLORS AND TEXTURES

Ask any experienced tourist about the best travel colors, and you'll hear similar answers. Dark, subdued colors that don't show dirt and that go with everything are first picks. Black is a favorite of many, but other darks such as navy, brown, and gray are popular too. Other travelers like to wear brighter, more colorful clothes. See the designer wardrobes, starting on page 38, for different approaches to color harmony on the road.

Regardless of the individual colors you use, it's smart to select a color theme as the basis for your core travel wardrobe. It's easier to create an adaptable wardrobe that is based

away; this means drying will be a breeze.

If you can't count on having access to an iron, steamer, or hot steamy shower, choose fabrics that either resist wrinkles or look fine even when wrinkled. Handwoven fabrics and moderate textures like tweeds, knits, and crepes show less wrinkling. Some cottons and most linens, while attractive fabrics to sew and wear, are famous for looking wrinkled. Leave them behind, unless you don't mind your clothes looking crumpled. If you really like the linen look for traveling, choose linen blended with cotton, silk, or rayon. Or shop for a linen "lookalike" fabric in some other fiber. To test for wrinkling, crumple a corner of the fabric for a few seconds before you cut into it; if the wrinkles don't relax right away, don't use the cloth for a travel garment.

on a single color or color family than a disparate collection of hues. It's most important that the individual items in your suitcase can intermingle in as many combinations as possible. This is easiest to achieve when all colors work well with each other.

Smooth or low-textured fabrics are good choices for travel garments, because they are lighter in weight and take up minimum luggage space. Such fabrics also layer more easily under and over other garments, an important consideration if you'll be spending time in environments with variable temperature. Smooth-textured garments won't catch or snag, so you won't have to worry about mending pulled threads or ripped hems.

Low-texture fabrics can provide some tactile interest to a smooth-surface outfit. Tweed, seersucker, pique, gauze, twill, and rib materials are subtly textured enough that they provide the lightweight, low-bulk characteristics of a smooth-surface

cloth, but have the additional advantage of disguising wrinkles and stains.

CARE CONSIDERATIONS

To spend as little on-the-road time as possible taking care of your clothing, be sure to note the care requirements of any fabric you buy for travel sewing. Look for materials that can be easily hand-washed and air-dried. Some of the high-tech fabrics are low-care because the cloth itself was designed to wick moisture

*U*sing especially eye-catching buttons on travel wardrobe items can relieve you of having to pack jewelry to accessorize your outfits. Buttons add the same pizzazz, but you won't have to worry about favorite pins or necklaces getting lost.

MARY PARKER, designer

*K*nit fabrics blended with Spandex are wonderful for traveling, because the elastic quality helps garments keep their shape and recover easily from wrinkling.

CATHY HAM, designer

Seasoned travelers expect a lot from their clothing while away from home. In addition to looking good, garments must be comfortable anywhere and any time, easy to wash in a hotel sink or basin of water, able to resist wrinkles even after a cramped 14-hour bus ride, and capable of defying the most persistent of stains. Luckily, the textile industry has developed many new-tech fabrics that make these feats possible.

From wicking moisture away from the skin to blocking drafty winds, today's materials help you put together a wayfaring wardrobe that meets all your on-the-road requirements. You've heard the trade-marked names, from Thinsulate to Supplex, and must wonder what they're made of and what they're good for. Here's a sampling of today's travel-friendly fibers to help you navigate the fabric shop, outfitter's store, travel catalog selections, and the world.

CoolMax. DuPont used its own Dacron fiber to create CoolMax, a high-performance porous fabric that moves sweat away from the body. This highly breathable material keeps the body cool and dry, and is used in many types of clothing, including sportswear, athletic and outdoor garments, bodywear, tights and socks, and sports bras.

Cordura. DuPont first developed this tough nylon fiber as a tire "cord" for "dura"bility (hence, the name), but it wasn't until scientists discovered how to dye the yarn that it found its way into consumer products in 1977. Cordura resists scuffs and tears, and is commonly found in backpacks, luggage and travel accessories, hiking shoes, and snowboarding and motorcycling apparel.

Dacron. A polyester cushioning fiber from DuPont that is used in many other applications, including CoolMax fabric and Fiberfill stuffing.

Gore-Tex. A waterproof, windproof, very breathable fabric system from W.L. Gore & Associates made from two different substances: an oleophobic or oil-hating substance that prevents penetration of contaminants and a hydrophobic or water-hating membrane that repels water droplets but allows water vapor or perspiration to escape. Gore-Tex is widely used in sports and outdoor apparel.

Hollofil. High-loft insulating fabric from DuPont used as an alternative to down.

Lycra. Spandex-based elastic fiber from DuPont that stretches five times its length, yet recovers to its original shape and size. Commonly used for athletic and active sports-

wear and often combined with other fibers for a form-fitting shape.

Polartec. A family of all-season fabrics from Malden Mills that provide warmth without weight, water resistance, and excellent moisture-wicking ability. Also known as Polar Fleece, this material comes in many weights and patterns, and is a pleasure to sew with. Polartec brand fabrics are made from polyester fibers; other brands may be polyester or acrylic.

Quallofil. High-loft insulating fabric from DuPont used as an alternative to down. Sometimes combined with antimicrobial elements to produce hypoallergenic products.

Supplex. A cotton-like fabric from DuPont that is made of fine-filament nylon for extra softness. It is breathable, odor-, wind-, and water-resistant, and won't wrinkle, shrink, or fade. When Supplex does get wet, it dries very quickly. It is commonly used in swimwear, exercise apparel, casual sportswear, and active sportswear.

Tactel. Nylon fiber from DuPont that provides a breathable suede-like finish to outerwear fabrics.

Teflon. Fluoropolymer finish from DuPont that repels soil, water, and oil. Used as a coating on non-stick

cookware in the 1960s, and today on outerwear fabrics.

Tencel. Recently developed fabric from British manufacturer Courtaulds Fibers that is derived from the natural cellulose in wood pulp. It is exceptionally strong, even when wet, and is increasingly being fashioned into soft, drapable yardage. Because Tencel is made from wood pulp rather than live trees, it is ecologically conservative in its use of natural resources. Tencel yardage is easy to sew and handles like a good quality rayon.

Thermolite. Insulating fabric from DuPont available in various lofts and weights.

Thinsulate. Insulating fabric of olefin and polyester from 3M Corporation. Its tangle of individual fibers creates insulating air space that reflects radiant body heat back to the body. Washable and dry-cleanable. Commonly used in jackets, parkas, and sleeping bags. Often combined with an outer layer that is waterproof and breathable, such as Gore-Tex or Supplex.

Ultrex. Densely woven fabric with microporous coating from Burlington that is waterproof, windproof, and breathable.

Velcro. Brand of hook-and-loop fasteners from Velcro Industries, named for the French words "velour" and "crochet." It's two-sided nature, with stiff hooks on one side and soft loops on the other, makes it a perfect choice for closures and fasteners of all kinds, from attaching shoulder pads to securing backpack flaps.

All fabrics are registered trademarks.

Recently, I was traveling by air and wanted to avoid packing a coat. I wore a decorative scarf around my neck along with a long sweater vest. I was plenty warm, and both the scarf and vest worked well with a variety of other outfits.

M. LUANNE CARSON,
designer

HANDWOVENS MAKE GOOD TRAVELING COMPANIONS

Handwoven fabrics, particularly woolens, are perfect for an on-the-road wardrobe. They are beautiful, out of the ordinary, and wrinkle- and stain-resistant. Tweed or multi-colored handwoven garments mix and match easily with other solid-colored and subtly patterned clothing. An added bonus is that fashions from hand-crafted fabrics attract admiring glances and are unique conversation-starters.

Susan Lilly of The Weaving Room in Corvallis, Oregon designs and weaves versatile, travel-friendly fashions, including jackets and full-length kimono-inspired coats. She finds that a short jacket, like the one shown here, is a great traveling companion. It looks good with jeans, khaki walking shorts, or a velvet skirt. It functions as a warm liner under a windbreaker or travel raincoat. And it is easy to make from a length of 20" (51 cm) handwoven cloth.

If you want to make something stylish out of your own handcrafted yardage or from some extra special handwoven material from your favorite fabric shop or craft studio, here's your chance. Susan shares the design for a version of her custom jacket, along with some general guidelines about sewing with handwoven fabrics.

HELPFUL HINTS FOR HANDWOVENS

▶ For a short jacket style, like the one shown here, begin with approximately 3½" yds (3.2 m) of handwoven wool yardage, at least 20" (51 cm) wide. Full the fabric in the washing machine in cool water on a gentle cycle, if it has not already been done. Roll the fabric in a towel to remove excess water, and then dry flat. Fulling (a textile term) sets the weave, plumps up the yarns, and softens the fabric. A stiff, scratchy handwoven wool will be amazingly soft and pliable after this pretreating step.

▶ Select a favorite loose-fitting garment, such as an unstructured jacket, tunic, or basic shirt (see Figure 1). Simplify the lines of the model

garment to conform with the loom-width of your handwoven fabric. Keep the general silhouette of the model garment, but redesign the component pieces and reconfigure seams to conform to the width of your fabric. For example, you may need to subdivide the garment back and front pieces to create side pieces. Figure 2 shows how the designer adapted a standard work shirt to coordinate with the 20" (51 cm) width of her handloomed fabric.

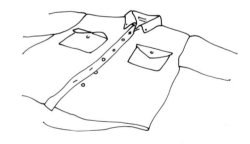

Figure 1

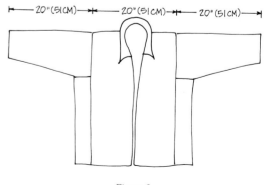

Figure 2

▶ Block out the idea for your adapted garment on graph paper. Create a paper pattern, using the fabric width and model garment shape as your guides. Add ½" (1.25 cm) seam allowances around each pattern piece. Be sure to take full advantage of selvages as finished edges where possible.

▶ Assemble a muslin sample garment, checking it for fit and drape. Make necessary changes to the muslin, and transfer changes to the paper pattern. Make a fresh paper pattern for each garment piece needed. Handwovens are cut from a single layer, with each piece cut out one at a time, so you will need separate pattern pieces for left and right components.

▶ Pin paper pattern pieces to the fabric. See Pattern Layout on the next page. Carefully cut out each piece and stack cut pieces for serging.

▶ Carefully serge all cut edges with a compatible color of thread. Set the serger to its widest 4-thread setting, with stitches close together.

▶ Cut facings and pockets from coordinating commercial yardage. Wool crepe works well with handwoven woolens.

CONSTRUCTION TIPS

From experience, Susan Lilly has developed these technical hints for ease of construction and a lightweight finished product. Bulky seams are eliminated by serging

edges before assembly and topstitching during assembly. To construct a short jacket from your handwoven yardage, start with the neckline and facing, working with the fabric flat.

1. If your jacket has a collar, pin the stitched and turned collar in place.

2. Press a ½" (1.25 cm) hem along the side edges of the facing, using the facing selvage as the finished edge along the back. See Figure 3.

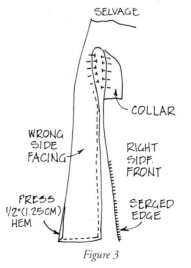

Figure 3

With right sides together, pin and stitch facing to jacket front in a ⅜" (1 cm) seam.

3. Clip curve and corners. Turn and press facing, using plenty of steam. Pin in place and topstitch all the way around. See Figure 4.

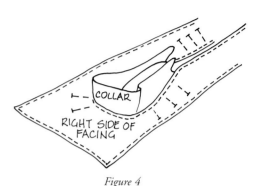

Figure 4

4. Attach sleeves by topstitching the jacket body to the sleeves, with the shoulder selvage of the sleeves placed ¼" (6 mm) under the selvage of the jacket body. See Figure 5. This produces a very lightweight, almost invisible dropped shoulder seam.

5. With right sides together, stitch underarm seams, only to the point where the side panels will be inserted (where underarm seam straightens out). Press open and topstitch

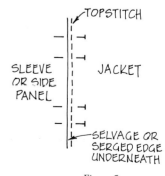

Figure 5

the serged edges in place. See Figure 6.

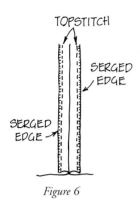

Figure 6

6. Stitch the remaining underarm seam to the selvage at the top of the side panel, lapping the selvage of the side panel over the serged edge of the underarm seam and top-stitching, to give a finished appearance to the inside of the jacket. See Figures 7 and 8.

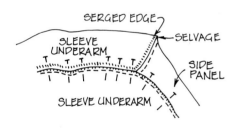

Figure 7

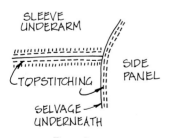

Figure 8

7. Stitch the remaining side panels in place by topstitching the selvage edges of the jacket body over the serged edges of the side panels, in the same manner that you stitched the sleeves and jacket body together.

8. Position pockets as desired along the side front seams. Stitch pocket straight edge along the serged seam allowance of the side panel; turn pocket toward front, press, and top-stitch along straight edge. Pin pocket in place and topstitch around the curved pocket edge. See Figure 9. Slit the jacket side seam to open the pocket.

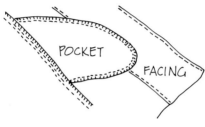

Figure 9

9. Turn up a narrow hem and top-stitch.

10. Finish jacket front with a zipper or decorative closure. Stitch in your custom label. See Figure 10.

11. Lightly press finished garment, using plenty of steam. Wear and enjoy!

Figure 10

PATTERN LAYOUT

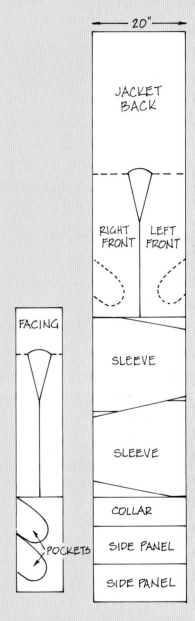

The design lines of a basic shirt jacket are simplified to conform to the 20"(51cm) width of the handwoven cloth. As a result, there is almost no waste and the selvage edges make clean-finished seams.

Being comfortable in your clothes is always desirable, but it's even more important when you travel. The days you spend traveling and away from home are very different than your everyday life, unless you travel for a living. You'll spend many more hours sitting, standing, and walking than you normally do. Your days will most likely be filled with more sightseeing, eating, and entertainment, and with less exercise than you're used to. So before you begin sewing, consider your itinerary, methods of travel, and time away from home. Then you can make adjustments to your selected patterns to guarantee comfort throughout the trip.

If your trip will include lots of walking, be sure to make skirts full enough to spread with your full walking stride. For straight skirts, make the back slit longer and insert a box pleat to keep your legs modestly covered. For wrap skirts, add walking ease so the wrapped panels won't separate while moving around (see page 41). Slacks should be loosely-fitted enough that the legs won't ride up as you walk.

BE KIND TO YOUR WAISTLINE

Weight variation is a fact of the traveling life. Waistline dimensions, in

particular, can change during travel time and long hours of sitting can cause ankles and feet to swell. Because of these vacillating changes in your figure, comfort will be very important to you, and you'll be glad you went for that "loose and layered" look for your journey. One of the great pleasures of traveling is sampling regional foods along the way. However, because it may be more difficult to keep up your exercise routine, your waistline will grow and your clothes can become uncomfortably tighter day by day. Plan ahead for this inevitable souvenir of your trip by building in some adjustability to your travel wardrobe and adapting sewing patterns to your specific needs.

Make your skirts adaptable by sewing wraparound fashions or styles that have adjustable waists. Elasticized waistlines in skirts and pants make them both comfortable and accommodating of gourmet adventures. Insert the elastic in the entire waistband, just in the back, or only at the sides, depending on the finished look you desire. Extra give in the waistline area can also be created with a drawstring, wrap-and-tie method, or adjustable buttons. See page 51 for a combination waistband on classic slacks that's kind to the traveler; it is slightly elasticized around the back and has buttoned tabs at the side that can be loosened or tightened as needed. Adjustable buckles can be purchased ready-made from sewing notions suppliers and inserted at the side waistline seams for adapting to daily needs. You may even want to insert a stretch tummy panel in slacks or skirts, to provide a little extra control.

ALL-TEMPERATURE WEAR

Temperatures can vary widely from location to location, and month to month. You may find yourself roasting on the airplane, but freezing in the terminal. Your itinerary may take you from the tropics to the chilly North, or simply from the blazing heat of outside to the air conditioned chill of inside. While you will select garment styles and fabrics for this temperature variability, you can also plan for it during clothing construction.

First, organize your wardrobe in layers so that every outfit is composed of elements that can be taken off or put back on as the temperature changes around you. Then you can go anywhere and know you'll be comfortable, as well as appropriately dressed for the environment. Consider incorporating detachable elements into garments, such as detachable sleeves, vest fronts, or skirt overlays. These change the look of garments and also add a bit of extra warmth. Button-in or zippered linings can turn a lightweight raincoat into a warm winter fashion, saving you the suitcase space of a separate coat or jacket. Consider lightweight fleece for pocket linings if you're heading north, but use airy batiste or a mesh fabric for hot-weather locales. In hot weather, mesh inserts in underarm and side seams can provide a little ventilation when the fabric spreads during normal movement.

PACKING IT ALL IN

Simple styles in lightweight fabrics will help you save luggage space, so look for patterns that have no collars or cuffs and that require minimal tailoring. Constructing garments with as few internal layers as possible makes them easier to pack in limited luggage space and wear with other clothing. Use the lightest weight interfacings possible, such as organdy, cotton batiste, or sheer

fusibles. Select pattern styles that have no interfacing at all and substitute bound edges or applied trim. Instead of self-fabric, use lightweight or mesh fabrics for plackets, facings, and undercollar. By reducing the weight and bulk of interior support fabrics, the finished garment will fold down to a compact size and be lightweight to wear.

EASY CARE FASHION

For garments that won't give you problems on the road, stitch or finish seams during construction so they won't ravel, ripple, or require pressing later. Topstitched, French, flat fell, and lapped seams all result in a finished look and don't need any further maintenance. You can also butt seams and cover the join with a decorative braid or bias strip; this results in a low-bulk, single-layer seam. If you prefer the speedy construction of serging, press the seams open or to one side and stitch down.

Choosing fabrics that resist or disguise wrinkles is the first step in creating a trouble-free travel wardrobe. You can also guard against wrinkles during garment construction by incorporating full or partial underlinings and linings. An underlining is a lightweight fabric that is cut out just like the fabric and basted to each fabric pattern piece; fabric and underlining are then handled as one during construction. This technique adds a bit of support to the fabric, prevents see-through, and reduces wrinkles. Full linings that are separately assembled and then sewn into the fabric garment also protect against wrinkles; a bonus of skirt linings is that they take the place of a slip. Partial linings, inserted into jacket sleeves and the knees of slacks, minimize the layers of fabric in the entire garment and help retain an unwrinkled appearance in areas of greatest movement and wear.

BUILT-IN SAFEGUARDS

Yet another reason to choose the "loose and layered" approach to travel fashion is that such garments easily accommodate hidden security features without upsetting the design silhouette. Before cutting out a garment, review the pattern for opportunities to incorporate hidden pockets, zippered compartments, secret panels, or detachable pocket totes. Make sure openings are securely fastened, and that buttons and snaps are securely sewed on.

Protect yourself from on-the-road repairs by stitching seams securely, and sewing closures on so they stay put. Don't forget to inconspicuously tack a spare button inside the garment, in case you lose one along the way. Stitch hems in short segments, knotting between each one, so a pulled thread doesn't cause the entire hem to unravel.

Assemble a small, portable mending kit like the one shown on page 119 and pack it in a corner of your bag. Enclose a few small spools of thread that coordinate with your wardrobe, along with some essential sewing notions. You'll be glad you brought it along in the event your clothing needs some mending, and if everything gets through your trip unscathed you'll at least have the security of knowing you were prepared for anything.

*U*se a variety of zippered mesh bags to carry on-board materials, such as knitting or sewing projects, books, or quick clean-up toiletries. This is especially helpful if you don't have easy access to your carry-on luggage during the trip. Just slip the mesh bag into the seat pocket as you get on board.

CATHY HAM,
designer

*K*eep your toiletry case packed and ready to go at a moment's notice, and restock it as soon as you get back home. You'll never be without an item that may be difficult to purchase elsewhere.

RONKE LUKE-BOONE,
designer

*I*f your feet swell after long hours of traveling, especially by air, wear lace-up shoes that can be easily loosened or tightened as needed.

M. LUANNE CARSON,
designer

SMOOTH SAILING

Once you've assembled the perfect travel wardrobe for your scheduled trip, you'll want to be sure that it gets there in good condition and works as well as you thought it would. If you carefully choose a selection of hard-working accessories before you leave, your core wardrobe will be beautifully enhanced. If you take the time to pack your clothes so that you get the most out of limited luggage space, you'll have everything you need. And if you un-pack as soon as possible after your arrival, your clothes will look the best they can for the duration. Finally, if you plan ahead for on-the-road repairs, you'll be prepared for anything, even if you're lucky enough to make it through an entire trip without losing so much as a button.

TO TRAVEL RIGHT, PACK LIGHT

It's amazing how much you can fit in a small, carry-on bag. Just attend a free packing demonstration offered by most travel or luggage stores, and you'll see item after item comfortably stowed in a modest suitcase when you were certain there couldn't be any more room. Granted, these are packing professionals, but you, too, can get everything you'll need in a small amount of space by following these basic packing tips:

▶ Arrange all of the items you're planning to take on the bed, and do a quick inventory to make sure everything is there. You want to be a lean and mean, unencumbered traveler, so use this opportunity to evaluate the overall wardrobe one last time and pare it down even more.

▶ Assemble a supply of dry-cleaning bags or tissue paper, to use as dividers between garments in the suitcase or to stuff sleeves or necklines to preserve garment shaping. The divider technique creates little air pockets that act as cushions to protect fabrics from wrinkling and from rubbing against each other in transit, which can cause pilling.

▶ Stow garments in a rolled-up rather than folded-up fashion, to cut down on creases. If you must fold, try to do it in the lower area of a garment, so you won't have creases right up front and center.

▶ Wrap items around each other, such as pants legs around a skirt or blouse sleeves around undergarments. This shapes the packed garments more gently and lessens their tendency to wrinkle.

▶ Use your scarves and shawls as "envelopes" to wrap around and protect other garments.

▶ Make assorted sizes of soft bags, like the Luggage Helpers on page 118, and use them to pack valuables or similar sizes and types of items. A larger bag can act as a "traveling dresser drawer" that you can transfer right into the hotel bureau upon your arrival.

▶ Pad collars with tissue or hosiery, to keep necklines from being crushed by other items.

▶ Stuff shoes with small, soft items, and pack shoes in bags to protect other garments from dirt and mud.

▶ Buckle belts one to another, and run them around the inside walls of the suitcase. Alternatively, roll them up tightly and stuff them in shoes.

▶ Pack an empty collapsible bag, such as the Fold-Flat Travel Tote on page 103, in the bottom of your suitcase so you'll have space for the treasures you bring home.

▶ Don't forget to take a special touch of comfort, such as a scented travel pillow like the one on page 00, a favorite photograph, or fragrant foot-soaking soap. Traveling can be hard on you, so plan ahead for some small ways to pamper yourself.

ON-THE-ROAD RX

If you took care to sew your travel garments securely, using seam finishing methods that won't ravel or require maintenance, your wardrobe should weather any voyage successfully. However, it always pays to be prepared for the unexpected accident. You might want to pack a small mending kit, such as the one shown on page 119, so you'll be able to make minor repairs to your clothes. Some spare buttons, a few safety pins, a needle, and loops of matching thread will take care of ripped seams, ragged hems, burst buttons, or splits and tears. In a pinch, you can even rely on double-stick tape for a temporary fix.

Guarding against stains is a bit more difficult, because you can't foresee environmental conditions. Selecting fabrics that won't show dust, dirt, or lint, and that are easy to launder, is

the first step to a low-maintenance travel wardrobe. When packing clothes to go, and when storing them en route, turn garments inside out so the right sides will be protected from stains and dust. This also helps preserve a wrinkle-free appearance, because creases facing to the inside are less obvious. If your clothing is dark-colored and you don't want to carry a lint brush, a small amount of masking tape or the double-stick tape you brought for emergency repairs will whisk away debris in a second.

AROUND-THE-WORLD FLAIR

The most basic travel wardrobe will appear as if you brought a closet full of fashions when spiced up with a small selection of interesting accessories, so give plenty of thought to how your individual garments can be accented. You have a lot to choose from, including vests, detachable collars and cuffs, jewelry, hats, gloves, belts and sashes, and the oh-so-versatile scarf. If you don't want to carry valuable jewelry, adorn some garments with sequins or other glittering decoration, or make soft-sculpture art jewelry from decorative cords, unusual buttons, feathers, or scraps of fabric and suede.

You will find the humble scarf to be the most essential ingredient for pulling together outfits in different ways. No one will notice you're wearing the same basic black dress four days in a row, when you spiff it up each time with an ethnic print sash tied around the hips, a floral print ascot around the neck, a beaded chiffon shawl draped around the shoulders, or several scarves knotted together end-to-end and worn as a belt. Because you love to sew, you will particularly enjoy collecting scarves because you can purchase as little as ¼ yd (.25 m) of any beautiful fabric and then turn it into a fashion accessory of the moment. Before long, you will have an entire wardrobe of scarves.

If you're all thumbs when it comes to tying a scarf in interesting ways, see "The Scarf: A Traveler's Best Friend" on this page for some easy variations. If you find a knotted variation you like but don't want to re-tie it every time, make a knot in one end of the scarf, rather than tying the two ends together; then attach to the other end with a small snap or dot of hook-and-loop tape. When wrapped and fastened, the scarf will always be tied just the way you like it. If you like a draped look, hand-tack the drapes in place so you will always be able to get the same look.

To keep a scarf from slipping and sliding out of place, simply pin it discreetly to the garment underneath. For a more permanent solution, stitch some loops to the back of the garment at the neckline or shoulder seam, as designer Joyce Cusick did on page 45. When the scarf stays put where it's meant to be, you look polished and stylishly put together all the time.

The Scarf:
A Traveler's Best Friend

A simple square or oblong of pretty fabric can be wrapped and tied in a number of ways, to transform any basic garment into a fabulous fashion.

A. SIMPLEST WRAP SASH

Fold a large square scarf in half diagonally to form a triangle. Wrap around waist or hips and knot the ends together.

B. CUSTOM OBLONG

To turn a large square (1) into an oblong shape, which is used to tie many imaginative knots, bring opposite corners into the center (2), and continue folding in the straight edges until you have the desired oblong size (3).

C. THE ROLLOVER

Fold a large square in half diagonally (1); wrap high around neck from front to back (2); bring ends to front and knot around middle of neck (3); roll upper fabric down over knotted ends (4).

D. CLASSIC SQUARE KNOT

Wrap scarf around neck, cross right end over left, and pull up through neck opening, top; cross left end over right and complete knot, bottom.

E. BOW ILLUSION

Start with an oblong and loosely knot it in the center (1); position knot at center front, wrap ends around neck, and bring to front (2); slip right end through knot from right to left (3); slip left end through knot, left to right (4).

F. CLASSIC NECKTIE

Adjust oblong around neck so left end is shorter than right (1); wind right end around left two times (2); slip right end up inside neck opening and over top of wrapped fabric (3); slip right end down through space between outer and inner loops, and pull firmly to make a knot (4); hold the left end and slide the knot up to tighten as desired (5).

G. THE TWIST

Wrap an oblong around your neck from back to front and twist ends around each other once (1); take ends to back of neck and knot (2).

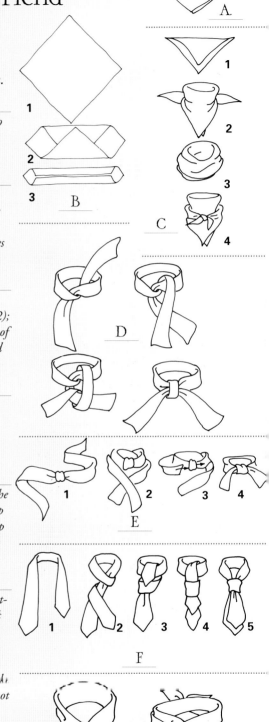

SUNGOLD WARDROBE

Designer ✳ Mary S. Parker

*B*righten up any cloudy corner of the world with this bright and beautiful grouping of coordinated clothes for dressy and casual wear. The designer gets the most mileage out of separates that have lots of mix-and-match possibilities—at least twenty different outfits out of twelve pieces.

This wardrobe will keep on looking good, no matter how many miles it travels. Fabric selections make on-the-road care easy; the silks and rayons wash out well in hotel sinks and steam well in hot showers. Skirts and slacks are lined and the suit was stabilized with fusible interfacing before cutting out, so the final garments resist sagging, bagging, wrinkling, and snagging. The long flowery mock-wrap skirt was lined using a straight skirt pattern, so that if the wind blows the skirt fronts apart, the fitted lining underneath preserves modesty.

For cooler climates or those in-between days, the microfiber raincoat has a lightweight washable insulated button-in lining. Layered over the suit or other garments, the coat provides comfort, warmth, wind and water resistance, and classy style wherever it goes. The designer added walking ease to the coat front, to make sure the fronts don't spread apart while walking or moving around (see illustration on page 41).

WARDROBE COMPONENTS

▶ Microfiber raincoat with button-in lining

▶ Suit with cardigan-style jacket and straight skirt in silk matka

▶ Mock-wrap skirt in rayon print

▶ Palazzo pants in rayon print

▶ Slacks in black silk matka

▶ Shirt jacket in rayon print

▶ Short-sleeved shawl-collar blouse in gold/white windowpane silk

▶ Long-sleeved high-neck blouse in gold/black/ivory silk print

▶ Short-sleeved mock turtleneck blouse in pale gold silk

▶ T-shirt in black/white houndstooth silk

▶ Sleeveless T-shirt in hot pink rayon

▶ Accessories: Long rayon print scarf, black belt, brooch, crushable straw hat

ALL-WEATHER COAT WITH BUTTON-IN LINER

Here's how to make a lining for a coat if your pattern doesn't include one. The coat shown here has a raglan sleeve that extends all the way to the neckline. The front facing is extremely wide, reaching all the way to the side seam. However, it extends around the neckline only as far as the sleeve front seam. There is no back facing or facing over the shoulder/sleeve area. To attach a removable lining, you will first need to construct facings for the back neck and shoulder/sleeve area. These will be sewn to the front facing to create a continuous area from which to "hang" the button-in lining.

Quilting the lining and insulation inside the back of the coat keeps the layers from shifting, and can be a pretty design detail, too, even though it doesn't show from the outside.

FOR COAT FACINGS

1. To make patterns for the new back and sleeve area facings, lay out the pattern pieces for the coat back and the two-part sleeve on a flat surface. Lay pattern or tracing paper on top.

2. Measure in from the neckline edge and mark a width equal to the front facing at the front sleeve seams. Trace a curving line, parallel to the neckline edge, through the marks you just made.

3. Incorporate these new facing pieces into the coat construction.

4. Sew buttons to the new facings, ¾" (2 cm) in from the neckline edge, at center back and at front and back sleeve seams.

5. Sew buttons to the front facings, ¾" (2 cm) in from the inside edges, from top to bottom, about 8" (20.5 cm) apart. You will make buttonholes in the edges of the lining to correspond to these buttons.

FOR COAT LINING

1. Use the coat front, back, and sleeve pieces as patterns, but make the following adjustments:

▶ Cut the lining for the back of the coat with the fold along the center back line, ignoring the back kick pleat. Also, cut off the seam allowance around the neck area and the hem allowance.

▶ Cut the lining for the front of the coat by folding back the front pattern piece along the center front line, cutting only the portion between center front and side seam. Also, cut off the seam allowance around the neck area and the hem allowance.

▶ Cut the lining for the sleeve the same as the pattern piece, but omit the seam allowance around the neck area and the hem allowance.

▶ Cut the insulating fabric the same as the lining fabric. Baste insulation pieces to the wrong side of the lining pieces around outer edges. Handle basted pieces as one during construction.

2. Assemble the coat lining and make buttonholes to match the buttons on the coat facings.

3. To ensure freedom of movement, slash the lining along the center back line from lower edge up about 10" (25.5 cm), and finish the raw edges to prevent raveling.

4. To prevent the lining fabric from sagging inside the back of the coat, quilt the lining/insulation in this area (see photo on page 40).

TO ADD WALKING EASE

1. Tape pattern or tracing paper to the center front edge of the coat front pattern piece.

2. Make a mark at center front, ⅝" (1.5 cm) down from the neck edge.

3. Place one end of a yardstick at the mark. Rotate the other end of the yardstick out, 1½" (4 cm) beyond center front, and make a mark. Draw a line connecting the marks.

4. Slide the yardstick along the line until its lower end is at the bottom edge of the pattern piece, and continue the line to the bottom edge (right).

5. You will use this new line as the cutting line for the center front. However, lay out the pattern piece according to the grainline as marked on the pattern, not according to the line you just drew.

6. You can alternatively slash and spread the pattern piece instead of adding to the center front edge (far right).

CENTER FRONT

CENTER FRONT

Designer Tips

▶ To help prevent puckering when sewing with microfiber, cut the fabric slightly off grain (10 percent or so) and use micro-tex needles.

▶ A quick and easy way to finish the outside edges of the coat facing and insulated liner is to bind them with double fold bias tape, or make your own bias binding out of complementary fabric. Purchase or make narrow bias for the coat fabric and wider bias for the thicker liner.

EGYPTIAN FANTASY WARDROBE

Designer ✳ Joyce E. Cusick

The designer has studied Egyptian art over the years and finds it a treasury of design inspiration. Museum exhibits and books have kept alive her fascination with all things Egyptian. When she encountered a new series of Egyptian print fabrics, the idea came to her for this versatile Fantasy Trip wardrobe. She says she can now travel to Egypt in her imagination until the day when the voyage becomes a reality.

This wardrobe's components all interact with each other in a number of ways, for visual interest and wearing flexibility. When combined with a few solid turquoise garments and a basic black grouping that includes dress, slacks, skirt, and short jacket, the possible outfits are multiplied even more. While the Egyptian print fabrics were interesting in themselves, Joyce was further inspired by them to enhance the wardrobe with creative touches, such as pleated edging and contrast bands (cut from one of the Egyptian print fabrics that had horizontal design motifs), a fabric neckpiece/collar, appliqué designs, Battenberg lace collar, decorative braid, and fun beaded necklaces.

WARDROBE COMPONENTS

Basic black garments

▶ Sleeveless dress, sleeveless top with Egyptian print appliqué on front

▶ Slacks, knee-length skirt

▶ Short jacket with drawstring waist and Egyptian print appliqué on back

Turquoise garments

▶ Slacks

▶ Shirt with Egyptian print yoke and decorative braid

Egyptian print garments

▶ Long wrap skirt, knee-length wrap skirt with contrast band along front opening edge, skorts with front panel

▶ Sleeveless sheath dress

▶ Sleeveless top with contrast bands

▶ Reversible short-sleeve jacket with pleated neckline edging and contrast bands (reverses to solid black)

▶ Gathered neckpiece/collar

Accessories

Sheer cotton shawl with tied fringe, black purse with Egyptian print appliqué and contrast bands, black Battenberg lace collar, assorted bead necklaces and jewelry

Appliqué Embellishments

By using the interesting motifs in the Egyptian print fabrics for the appliqué designs, Joyce created
special touches on several of the garments (including one store-bought T-shirt) that then coordinated perfectly with the entire wardrobe. She simply applied a fusible web product to the wrong side of a scrap of the print fabric, cut out a complete design motif, peeled the backing off the fusible web product, and then fused the appliqué shape to the cut-out garment piece. She then stitched around all outside edges of the appliqué shape in satin stitch and machine embroidery thread.

This Battenberg lace collar is a unique accessory and guaranteed conversation piece.

By pleating the Egyptian print fabric for a neckline edging band, the designer achieved an attractive dimensional effect.

To keep scarves draped correctly around her neckline, the designer adds these handy loops at center back.

EGYPTIAN PRINT
NECKPIECE/COLLAR

*T*he ancient Egyptians wore wide collars to protect their shoulders
from the hot sun, and often embellished them with embroidered
bands or braid. This attractive fabric collar is easy to make, goes
with many different garments, and can be decorated as you please.

Figure 2

MATERIALS

▶ ¼ yd (.25 m) print fabric of choice, 45" (115 cm) wide, plus scrap for bias strip

▶ 1½ yds (1.4 m) narrow braid

▶ 3 yds (2.75 m) braid edging

▶ Fabric glue (optional)

INSTRUCTIONS

1. Cut three strips of fabric, 3" by 45" (7.5 by 115 cm), for collar.

2. Cut one bias strip of fabric, 2" by 20" (5 by 51 cm), for neckline binding.

3. Stitch two collar strips together end-to-end, finish seams, and press open. See Figure 1.

4. Finish all raw edges, by serging, overcasting, or binding.

5. Stitch along top edges of both collar strips, using long stitches and leaving thread tails hanging at both ends (you will gather these edges); stitch again ¼" (6 mm) away in seam allowance.

6. Gather top edges of both strips. Lap shorter strip over gathered edge of longer strip and stitch in place. Trim close to stitching. Adjust gathers at neck edge for a comfortable fit and attach bias strip, leaving tails of bias strip to tie collar behind neck. See Figure 2.

7. Stitch braid on top of seams and braid edging along lower edge.

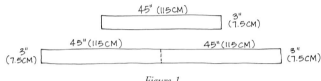

Figure 1

EASY-SEW SHAWL WITH TIED FRINGE

Make a custom accessory with any coordinating fabric that is lightweight and sheer enough to drape around the shoulders. The decorative fringe is easy to do—simply unravel some threads and tie square knots.

INSTRUCTIONS

1. Cut a piece of gauze, voile, or sheer linen 28" (71 cm) wide and 3 yds (2.75 m) long.

2. Measure 3" (7.5 cm) from each end and draw out a crosswise thread. Stitch across the scarf where the thread has been removed on each end.

3. Make a narrow hem on both long edges.

4. Unravel/draw out the 3" (7.5 cm) of crosswise threads from each end for the fringe.

5. Separate the threads into groups of about ⅜" (1 cm) wide. Tie adjacent groups in a square knot (right over left, left over right). For the second row of knots, tie one set of threads from each knot in the previous row. Repeat for third row (see

A length of soft, sheer fabric makes a pretty shawl when unraveled and knotted at the ends.

illustration above). For a 4-yd (3.7-m) scarf, make fringe 4" (10 cm) long and tie four rows of knots. Trim all fringed ends to an equal length.

FABULOUS
FALL WARDROBE
Designer ✳ Joyce Baldwin

*T*his mix-and-match collection of garments can be dressed up or down for any occasion and is comfortable to wear in cool, warm, or wet weather. The vest and ikat print over-shirt can be layered over other garments for interest, temperature comfort, or to build interesting outfits. The basic beige, brown, and black colors set off the red accent color and graphic designs beautifully. And the hand-crafted jewelry highlights the creativity of this designer.

For traveling comfort, Joyce adapted the waistband design of the beige and black checked slacks to adjust in or out as needed, so she would be comfortable while traveling and while sampling the cosmopolitan fare. And for security, she hid three pockets inside the checked jacket. One small pocket is set inside a larger pocket for double layer protection of passport, travelers' checks, or other valuables.

Wardrobe Components

▶ Jacket and slacks in beige/black checked linen blend

▶ Jacket and slacks in black cotton blend

▶ Slacks in red gabardine

▶ Walking shorts in red corduroy

▶ Walking shorts in khaki cotton blend

▶ Skirt and blouse in black/white/red print silk blend

▶ Blouse with button-on jabot in black crinkle cotton

▶ Graphic print overshirt in black/white ikat with red accents

(modeled after a fabric arrangement by Mary Parker)

▶ Quilted reversible vest in black/tan/bronze cotton print

▶ T-shirts in black, red, and khaki cotton knit

▶ Accessories: Large red/black/white scarf to wear as sarong, halter top, shawl, or sash; small red and black chiffon scarves; straw hats; assorted bangle bracelets and ethnic bead necklaces; lightweight red rain poncho

Easy Button-On Jabot

A classic blouse is made just a tad dressier by a scarf, ascot, or jabot and this self-fabric version adds a

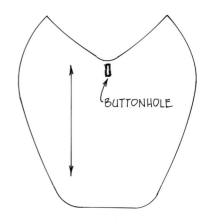

Make a quick blouse accessory out of leftover fabric. Cut the shape shown here on the lengthwise grain; turn under edges and narrow hem. Then make a buttonhole that fits the blouse buttons.

subtle touch. It couldn't be simpler to make, and therefore saves the time and money of searching for the right neckline accessory. Out of a scrap of the blouse fabric, cut a single layer along the lengthwise grain, in the shape shown in the illustration. Turn under and stitch a narrow hem all around, and then make a buttonhole that fits the buttons on the blouse. Attach the jabot at the neckline or the next button down, to fit under a pretty necklace of pearls or silver beads.

EXPANDABLE WAISTBAND

When you travel by air, waistlines tend to swell right along with feet, and continue to swell after you arrive at your destination because of away-from-home exercise and eating habits. Lots of travel clothes have elastic waistlines, but their obviously "gathered" appearance can look bulky and unflattering. This nifty alteration preserves the sleek look of slacks and skirts, and builds in comfort that can adjust to your daily needs. For maximum comfort, combine these adjustable side belts with elastic in

Customizing a pair of pants with these adjustable side belts means maximum comfort wherever you go.

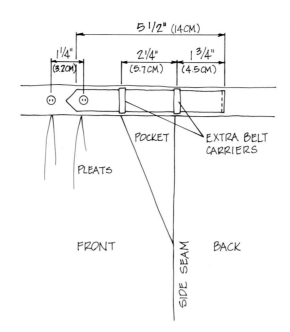

the back waistband. Here's how to do it:

1. Increase the waist size of pants or skirt pattern by 1" to 1½" (2.5 to 4 cm). You can make this increase at the side seams or center back seam, by decreasing dart or pleat size, or by eliminating one of the multiple pleats, depending on the garment style. The increase can also be distributed among several of these locations. NOTE: If the hip area of the garment fits snugly, you may want to increase the hip size as well, by as much as 1" (2.5 cm).

2. Lengthen waistband pattern by same amount of waist increase alteration.

3. Make pattern for "quarter" belt sections. The finished width of these short belts should be a little narrower than the garment waistband. The permanently attached belts ends should be square; the adjustable ends can be square or pointed. The finished length of the belts (one on

each side of the garment) should be 5" to 6" (12.5 to 15 cm) long, depending on wearer's waist size. See illustration.

4. Cut out the belt pieces and interface them, to provide stability for the buttonholes. Stitch, trim, turn, and press belts. Make buttonholes near the shaped ends.

5. Cut out at least two extra belt carriers and add them to each side area of the pants, for the short belts to pass through. If other belt carriers are called for by the pattern, you may have to redistribute their spacing to accommodate the extra carriers.

6. Pin belts to waistband and adjust position as desired; stitch to waistband at side back area.

7. Sew sets of two or three buttons to each side front waistband, at the desired spacing. The short belts can be buttoned as needed to adjust waistband fullness.

BROADWAY BOOGIE WARDROBE

Designer ✱ Mary S. Parker

A scheduled trip to New York City for theater-going and club-hopping inspired this glamorous but hard-working wardrobe of reversibles and interchangeables. The color scheme is elegant black studded with the neon colors of flashing nighttime lights.

The designer chose comfortable pattern styles with plenty of wearing ease, a benefit for a trip with hours of sitting, eating, and drinking. She maximized comfort even more with elasticized waists and tunic blouses that don't have to be tucked in. The fabrics she selected—drapey crushable silks and silk blends—were appropriately dressy, comfortable, easy care, warm when layered, and wrinkle-resistant.

WARDROBE COMPONENTS

▶ Reversible pull-on palazzo pants and unstructured jacket, black charmeuse on one side and printed with a brightly-colored Japanese temari ball pattern on the other

▶ Reversible pull-on palazzo pants, black charmeuse on one side and black chiffon on the other

▶ Reversible jacket with draped lapels, black and turquoise polka dot charmeuse on one side and turquoise on the other

▶ Japanese-inspired jacket, black cut velvet chiffon

▶ Short-sleeved pullover blouse, black and turquoise polka dot charmeuse

▶ Four-way reversible sleeveless tunic, violet/fuchsia on one side and scarlet/royal blue on the other

▶ Camisole top, black charmeuse

▶ Accessories: Bead belt to wear over four-way tunic

Four-Way Reversible Tunic

This easy fashion is like having four different blouses in one, with the colors changing from inside to out and front to back. It's nearly a full week's worth of tops to wear with jacket and pants or skirt. Any sleeveless pullover blouse pattern will work. Here's how:

1. Check your blouse pattern to make sure that the blouse front is at least as wide as the back in the bust and hip areas. If it is not, add to the front side seams to make it as wide as the blouse back. Cut four blouse fronts from assorted fabrics. Pin and stitch two of the fronts, right sides together, at the shoulders. Repeat with other two fronts. Press seams open.

2. With right sides together, pin and stitch the two sets together around the neckline edge. Clip seam, turn garment to right side, and press well.

3. Pin right sides of one armhole seam together, while leaving the garment turned to the right side in the neck seam area. This is a little tricky. Scrunch up the neck seam area and opposite armhole, so you can pin the right sides of the armhole together around the scrunched-up fabric; the stitched armhole forms a tunnel around the neck opening and opposite armhole. Clip and trim seam allowance; turn right side out through the "tunnel," and press gently. Repeat with the other armhole seam.

4. With right sides together, sew sides of the blouse in a continuous seam, from the hem of one color combination, up past the armhole, and down to the hem of the other color combination. Turn to right side through shoulder. Press well.

5. Turn up hems and baste in place; trim hem seam allowances to 3/8" (1 cm). With wrong sides together, edgestitch around entire hem through all layers. Press well.

Designer tips for reversible pants and jacket

▶ Reversible pants with an elasticized waist are the ultimate in comfort and convenience. Simply sew the two completed pants together, right sides together, along the actual waistline; trim, turn, and press. Topstitch very close to the waistline edge, to keep the layers from shifting. Then sew the pants together, wrong sides together, down from the waistline the width of your elastic; this forms the casing through which you will insert the elastic.

▶ To make sure the pants hang straight, tack the crotch seams together for about 1" (2.5 cm) at the four-way intersection point, carefully matching the seams up with one another.

▶ Hem each pants layer separately, so both layers will hang straight. You may want to hem one layer slightly longer than the other, rather than trying to match up the hem edges exactly and risking the reverse layer peeking out at random spots.

▶ For a reversible jacket fashion, choose a pattern that does not require shoulder pads. If you look best with shoulder pads, then incorporate them into the garments you wear underneath the jacket.

▶ Stay away from jackets with lapels, unless you don't mind having the "inside" fabric visible in the lapel turn-back area.

▶ To make sure the jacket hangs straight, no matter which side is showing, tack the underarm seams together for about 1" (2.5 cm) at the four-way intersection point.

The designer hemmed the solid black side of these reversible palazzo pants a tiny bit longer than the print side, so bright spots of color wouldn't peek out at the hemline when she wears the black side out.

SPRING GARDEN

Designer ✳ Joyce E. Cusick

*T*his colorful bouquet of garments is bright, fresh, and flexible. The individual components can be layered or not, depending on the temperature, making this a perfect wardrobe for transitional, in-between seasons or for a trip that takes you from cool to warm locations. The options for mixing prints and solids are numerous, for a complete wardrobe that can be worn for all occasions—dressy, casual, or fun.

WARDROBE COMPONENTS

▶ Six-yard wardrobe of lined jacket, sleeveless dress, skirt, and slacks in royal blue

▶ Unlined sheath dress and overshirt in multi-colored print

▶ Skirt, shorts, long-sleeve blouse, and sleeveless blouse-jacket in blue/gray/white print challis

▶ Accessories: brooch, pearls, white lace scarf, blue scarf, blue and red straw hats

YES, YOU CAN PACK A HAT

If your heart is set on taking along a straw hat or other firmly shaped chapeau, you don't have to wear it on the plane. You can pack a hat right in your luggage, with these tips from hat-lover Joyce Cusick.

▶ Line the bottom of a large suitcase with a 1" (2.5 cm) layer of underthings and lingerie.

▶ Cut a strip of cardboard or heavy paper long enough to wrap around the crown of the hat, and tape the ends together.

▶ Lay cardboard circle in center of suitcase.

▶ Pack other items around it, keeping shoes near the back of the case.

▶ Turn hat upside down and position crown down into cardboard circle.

▶ Stuff crown with soft or small items.

▶ Cover the hat and packed items with a double layer of tissue paper.

▶ Pack skirts, slacks, and blouses on top, divided by layers of tissue paper. Tissue protects garments from wrinkling and also functions as convenient trays for lifting out layers of clothing.

THE SIX-YARD WARDROBE

Designer Joyce Cusick has a busy life that includes lots of travel both for pleasure and business. She also loves to keep an eye out for special fabrics wherever she goes. She developed a "six-yard wardrobe" approach to travel sewing after several trips to the local fabric store for more of the same material. She started with enough of the royal blue linen blend shown on these pages to make the skirt and slacks. She liked working with the fabric so much that she went back twice for more, to make the jacket and then the dress. The garments have become a well-traveled all-weather wardrobe and she reports that she's worn them in various combinations at least three hundred times!

Joyce realized that if she consistently bought 6 yards (5.5 m) of 45" (115 cm) or 60" (152 cm) solid color fabric, she would always have enough to sew a complete basic wardrobe that includes jacket, slacks, skirt, top, and sometimes a dress. Knowing this ahead of time makes it easy and fun to shop for fabric. She doesn't have to know precisely how much to buy of a good find at the fabric store or street market, but she's always sure that there will be enough to make up a well-coordinated grouping of versatile garments. Today, all of her travel clothes are created from six-yard wardrobes, plus a few print accent garments and an assortment of accessories.

DRESS UP
ANY SEASON

Designer ✳ Joyce E. Cusick

*T*his classy ensemble includes one of the designer's six-yard wardrobes, plus one special accent garment and a few accessories. The group of five core items is perfect for a business trip that will include some dress-up occasions, from an evening at the theatre to an embassy ball. All of the individual garments also mix and match nicely with another six-yard wardrobe in black fabrics.

WARDROBE COMPONENTS

▶ Six-yard wardrobe of lined jacket, skirt, slacks, and slip dress in royal blue

▶ Lace sheath dress to wear over slip dress

▶ Accessories: Lace scarf in natural white, pearls

WORKING WITH LACE

Sewing a simple dress from lace fabric is an easy way to create an extra special fashion. The lace, all by itself, creates a dressed-up look, so no other embellishment or accessorizing is needed. And this heavier weight lace drapes nicely and needs no underlining or support. By making a lace dress to wear over a silk chemise or slip dress, you end up with a versatile duet of pretty dresses without sacrificing the romantic see-through quality of the lace. Here are some tips from the designer for working with lace:

▶ Select a lace fabric that has a pretty scalloped or "galloon" edge and use it for its decorative effect. Cut the dress sleeve, front, and back pieces so the actual hemline is positioned along the shaped edge of the fabric. No further hem finishing is required and the undulating effect is beautiful.

▶ To create the same pretty scalloped effect at the neckline, cut a 2-3" (5-7.5 cm) strip from the remaining galloon edge of the fabric, following the design motif of the lace. Fit the strip around the finished neckline of the dress and stitch along the lines of the lace pattern. Trim away excess lace below the line of stitching.

CROSS-SEASON WARDROBE
Designer ✳ Joyce E. Cusick

*I*n Joyce's career as a Historic Preservation Specialist, she travels everywhere to evaluate historic properties and buildings. She attends countless meetings and spends many hours out in the field, a schedule that requires both a professional and comfortable wardrobe. This collection helps her stay comfortable and look good in many locations at any time of year. The checked English wool blazer has been to London, Scotland, Quebec, New York City, New Orleans, Charleston, and other U.S. cites as well as more casual locations. It looks great dressed up with skirt and blouse, or dressed down with velvet jeans and silk T-shirt.

WARDROBE COMPONENTS

▶ Six-yard wardrobe of lined jacket, sleeveless dress, skirt, and slacks, in pale blue linen/polyester

▶ Blouse and skirt in blue/beige/ivory print challis

▶ Lined jacket in beige/green/teal English wool

▶ Slacks and skirt in dark green lightweight wool

▶ Slacks and skirt in beige lightweight wool

▶ Slacks in teal wool

▶ Two tapestry print vests to coordinate with all other garments

▶ Accessories: Brooch, pearls, print scarf, lace scarf

TAPESTRY PRINTS FOR ON-THE-ROAD VERSATILITY

Walking into the upholstery or drapery department of a fabric store can be dizzying because of the hundreds of beautiful prints, patterns, and colors. While these fabrics are too heavy and stiff for many garment styles, they can be attractively used in some instances, such as the vest fronts that Joyce used in her travel wardrobe. The heavy weight of the tapestry fabric provides a layer of warmth, either when worn by itself or under a jacket, but because the vest back is made from lining fabric, the overall garment isn't too bulky or stiff. So, if you just cannot resist those beautiful tapestry prints, follow these tips from the designer for successful sewing:

▶ Make sure you choose a fabric that has not been backed with latex or any other treatment. These backed fabrics just are not appropriate for wearables.

▶ Prewash the fabric before you cut

into it, to see how soft and pliable it will become. You can always ask for some samples from the fabric store and prewash all of them, then go back and purchase those that come out of the wash with the desired results.

▶ Choose lightweight interfacings and lining fabrics, so the finished garment won't be too hefty. You may not even need interfacing, because upholstery and drapery fabrics have so much body themselves.

▶ If you're making an unlined garment, finish the raw seam edges without adding bulk. Use a method, such as serging or overcasting, that doesn't require folding the raw edge under.

▶ Be diligent about pressing as you sew, to flatten seams and reduce bulk in the finished garment.

HAPPY PATCHWORK JACKET

Designed by Karen M. Bennett

Let the colors go wild and your imagination soar in this reversible jacket that looks equally inspiring on both sides.

Materials and Tools

▶ Pattern for bolero-style or short jacket

▶ 3 yds (2.75 m) cotton fabric for non-patchwork side

▶ 3 yds (2.75 m) cotton flannel, for interlining

▶ ¼-⅓ yd (.25-.33 m) each of twelve different cotton fabrics, or a variety of scraps, for patchwork side

▶ Coordinating rayon embroidery thread or other decorative thread for appliqué

▶ Metallic thread and appropriate sewing machine needle for free-motion quilting

▶ Machine darning or quilting foot, zipper foot

▶ 10 yds (9.15 m) cord for piping

▶ Fusible stabilizer of choice

▶ Tracing paper for appliqués

▶ Tailor's soap or other marking product

▶ Teflon pressing sheet

▶ Notions required by pattern

Instructions

1. Prewash all fabrics. Flannel can shrink quite a lot, so you may want to prewash it twice.

2. For non-patchwork side, place pattern pieces on fabric and trace around outside edges with tailor's soap or other marking product. Don't forget to reverse front and sleeve pattern pieces, for right and left sides. Do not cut pattern pieces out until the machine quilting is completed.

3. Layer non-patchwork fabric and flannel, and pin or baste together.

4. With metallic thread, machine darning or quilting foot, and appropriate sewing machine needle, drop machine feed dogs and free-form quilt fabric/flannel fronts, back, and sleeves in a random pattern. Start from edges of pieces and avoid stitching on top of previous stitched lines.

5. Cut pattern pieces out of quilted fabric and, with regular sewing thread, stitch ⅛" (3 mm) from all edges to secure metallic threads.

6. For patchwork side, cut rectangles from assorted fabrics and piece together into strips that are a little longer than the pattern pieces; stitch in ⅛-¼" (3-6 mm) seams. The designer cut two sizes of rectangles, 4½" x 5½" (11.5 x 14 cm) and 4½" x 2½" (11.5 x 6.5 cm), and alternated them. See Figure 1. Press all seams to one side as you go.

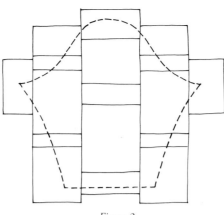

Figure 2
Adding rectangles at sides for sleeve pieces

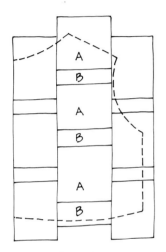

A: 4½"x 5½" (10 X 12.5 CM)
B: 4½"x 2½" (10 x 6.5 CM)

Figure 1
Patchwork fabric for front pattern piece

7. For jacket fronts, sew three strips together, offsetting the center strip. See Figure 1. Add rectangles at sides, as needed for width. Compare pieced fabric to front pattern, to be sure you will have enough to cut out the pattern.

8. For jacket back, sew five strips together, offsetting center and outside strips, and adding rectangles at sides, as needed for width. Compare pieced fabric to back pattern, to be sure you will have enough to cut out the pattern.

9. For jacket sleeves, sew three strips together, adding rectangles as needed for width at sleeve cap and around armhole. See Figure 2. Compare pieced fabric to sleeve pattern, to be sure you will have enough to cut out the pattern. See Designer Tip on next page.

10. Cut pattern pieces out of patchwork fabric and stitch ⅛" (3 mm) from all edges, to secure threads and seams.

11. Apply fusible stabilizer to wrong side of assorted fabrics for appliqué shapes. Trace desired shape onto fabrics and cut out.

12. Arrange appliqué shapes onto patchwork fronts, back, and sleeves; fuse into place.

13. Satin stitch around edges of appliqué shapes with rayon embroidery thread. Pull thread tails to wrong side and tie off.

14. Begin assembly of non-patchwork and patchwork jackets separately, according to pattern instructions.

15. To make piping, cover cord with

▶ When piecing the fabric strips for the sleeves, don't make a huge square of fabric, because you'll waste a lot of your hard work once you cut the sleeves out. Instead, shape the overall patchwork as you go to conform to the shape of the sleeve pattern. See Figure 2 on page 65.

▶ Sew the two jackets together with the patchwork side up, to make sure all seam allowances are stitched down facing the right direction.

▶ Because I can't attach my designer label to a reversible garment, I like to sign my name somewhere on the garment in free-motion quilting. This adds a distinctive touch!

▶ Here's a great tip for making your own piping, thanks to dressmaker Elizabeth Searle of Asheville, North Carolina. Cut the bias fabric strip at least 2" (5 cm) wide. Double the length of cord you need and add 2" (5 cm); for example, if you need a finished length of piping of 12" (30.5 cm), cut the cord 26" (66 cm) long. Wrap the bias around the right-hand half of the cord. Sew one short end of the bias, stitching across the cord; pivot at outside edge and begin stitching long edge of bias, quickly tapering toward the encased cord and gently stretching the bias as you sew. See Figure 3 below. Trim seam allowance close to stitching. To turn piping right side out, begin at wide end of bias and gently slide bias tube from right-hand half of cord to left-hand half; the widened end of the bias makes it easier to begin the turn. Trim off excess right-hand half of cord.

Figure 3
Encasing cord for piping

fabric of choice; baste piping along seamlines of neck, front opening, and hems of non-patchwork jacket.

16. For button loops, cut pieces of piping 3½" (9 cm) long; fold in half and baste to front seamline at desired locations.

17. Slide one jacket into the other, right sides together, and use a zipper foot to sew around neck and front opening edges, leaving an opening large enough to turn the assembled jackets right side out.

18. Trim seam allowances, clip curves, and turn jacket right side out. Press carefully, using the Teflon pressing sheet on the machine-quilted side to avoid melting or burning the metallic thread.

19. Slip stitch opening and sleeve hems closed.

20. Make and attach buttons of choice. The designer used narrow bias tubes of the various fabrics to make ball buttons.

BEVY OF BLUES REVERSIBLE VEST
Designed by Mary Russell

Express your creative spirit twice over in this reversible fashion that will extend your travel wardrobe.

67

Materials and Tools

▶ Pattern for simple vest with no darts

▶ At least nine different fabrics for each side, ¼ yd (.25 m) of each, or large scraps of assorted fabrics

▶ Cotton batiste, in amount of yardage required by pattern

▶ Measuring and marking tools

▶ Notions required by pattern

Instructions

1. Cut out the vest pattern pieces from the batiste, to form a foundation to which you will sew the patchwork fabrics. It is recommended that you cut each piece slightly larger than the pattern tissue, and then trim to actual size after adding the patchwork.

2. One side of the vest is made by assembling custom yardage from various sizes of rectangles, squares, and strips. You may piece a length of custom yardage, or piece three separate rectangles for the vest fronts and back. Cut out the vest pattern pieces from finished yardage.

3. The reverse side of the vest is a collage of curving and shaped pieces of fabric. Cut fabric shapes as desired and place on top of batiste foundation until it is completely covered, rearranging shapes as needed to get a pleasing composition. Cover the raw edges with straight or curving strips of fabric and stitch through all layers. Cut out the vest pattern pieces from collaged yardage.

4. Assemble vest according to pattern instructions, substituting one of the custom pieced layers for the vest lining.

Designer Tip

▶ When choosing fabrics for a pieced composition, try to unify them according to a "theme," such as related colors or pattern motifs. Keep in mind the colors and designs of the garments you will wear the vest with, for a versatile and balanced wardrobe.

TWO-IN-ONE JACKET AND HAT

Designed by Fradele Feld

A *reversible quilted jacket pro-*
vides double the good looks, and its
matching hat is a stylish finishing
touch that keeps your ears warm, too.

Materials and Tools

▶ Pattern for simple, loose-fitting jacket with set-in sleeves

▶ Pattern for pillbox hat

▶ Two fabrics of choice, as required by pattern, plus 1 yd (.95 m) for hat and bias piping around edges of jacket. Selected a medium to large print for one side, and a coordinating solid color or small print for the other side (the small print should "read" as a solid).

▶ Batting in a weight suitable for clothing

▶ Thread in neutral or coordinating color, plus optional decorative, variegated, or metallic thread for quilting

▶ Approximately 4½-5 yds (4.15-4.6 m) cording

▶ Tissue or tracing paper for making pattern alterations

▶ Marking and cutting tools

▶ Zipper foot, darning foot, open-toe foot for sewing machine

▶ Notions required by pattern

Machine quilting adds a decorative touch and keeps the layers of fabric from shifting.

Instructions

1. Make desired alterations to pattern, using tissue or pattern paper. For example, you might want to add extensions to the upper front jacket opening (see Figure 1). One side of the jacket will then lap completely over the other when you need extra

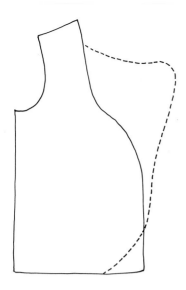

Figure 1
Add an extension to one jacket front for a warm overlap and also a nice touch of contrast when worn back like a lapel. Round off the corners at the front hem edge, so it will be easier to add the piping in a smooth, curving line.

warmth; when worn turned back, as lapels, the extensions attractively show off the reverse fabric. Round off any sharp corners at the neck or lapels, to make it easier to add the piping.

2. If you desire pockets, make a pattern large enough to fit your hands and determine placement on the jacket pattern pieces.

3. Cut altered pattern from both fabrics and the batting.

4. Trace desired quilting pattern and transfer to solid fabric sleeve pieces. Layer solid fabric sleeve pieces on top of batting and machine quilt the traced pattern. This will hold the batting in place inside the sleeves once the jacket is constructed.

5. Layer printed fabric front and back pieces on top of batting and free-motion quilt along the design lines of the fabric pattern in several areas, to hold the batting firmly in place.

6. Begin construction of both jackets, according to pattern directions, adding pockets to side seams if desired. See Tips for Reversible Garments on page 22.

7. To make piping, cut bias strips of either fabric 1½-2" (4-5 cm) wide and long enough to go around neckline, front, and hem edges of jacket. Save any extra for hat. Wrap bias strip around cording and baste with zipper foot; sew over cording with contrasting thread and decorative stitch, if desired.

8. Baste piping along seamline of solid fabric, starting and ending at a side seam. When sewing jackets together, right sides together, be sure piping is sandwiched in between; use a zipper foot to be sure stitching is close to cording. Leave an unstitched opening large enough to turn jackets right side out.

9. Complete jacket construction. Machine quilt around several designs on printed fabric as above, through all layers, avoiding pocket areas. If desired, channel quilt several rows around bottom edge and at bottom of sleeves, to hold layers in place.

For the Hat:

1. If your hat pattern does not have an ear-warmer flap, make your own pattern for it. Measure around the bottom edge of the hat pattern to determine how long the flap should be; it should cover your ears and extend around the back of your head when turned down. The length of the flap will probably be about 3" (7.5 cm) shorter than the bottom edge of the hat and the width of the flap should be about 3" (7.5 cm) at the center back, tapering as desired toward the front. See Figure 2.

2. Cut hat and flap patterns from both fabrics and batting.

3. Baste leftover piping to outer seamline of one flap.

4. Layer flaps right sides together and stitch around outer edge; trim seams, turn right side out, and press.

5. Machine quilt flap along design

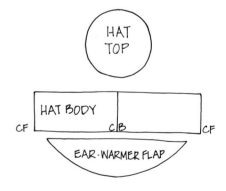

Figure 2
Make a pattern for an ear-warmer flap by cutting it a bit shorter than the hat body pattern, so the flap won't cover your eyes when turned down. Make sure the flap is wide enough to completely cover your ears, tapering as it extends around to the front.

"I wanted a jacket that would be versatile enough to go with a lot of other garments. I chose printed fabric in favorite colors for the more flamboyant side, and a toned down print for a more conservative look. The matching hat helps me look dressed up, and really keeps me warm in chilly weather."

lines of print fabric, as desired, to hold layers together.

6. Begin construction of hat body, according to pattern directions. Be sure to sandwich the flap between the two layers along the bottom edge, with the midpoint of the flap at the center back seam of the hat body.

7. Machine quilt hat body to coordinate with jacket.

8. Layer the top of the hat, right sides facing out with batting in between; machine quilt as before.

9. Cut a bias strip long enough to go around top of hat, plus seam allowances; press under seam allowance along one long edge. Baste unpressed edge around outside edge of hat top.

10. Stitch hat top to hat body; trim seam allowance. Turn pressed edge of bias strip over seam allowance and stitch close to edge.

Designer Tips

▶ If your sewing machine has a darning foot or open-toe foot, use it for the quilting. A darning foot helps you keep control and maintain even stitching lines, and an open-toe foot makes it easier to see where you're going.

▶ Add an unusual touch to your custom piping by sewing a decorative stitch over the wrapped cording with a metallic or decorative thread. The blind hem stitch makes a very nice pattern over the piping.

▶ When sewing the two jackets together, position the solid fabric on top so you don't have to stitch on the batting side. This makes it easier to see your stitches.

FOUR SEASONS VESTS

Designed by Denise Glick

Choose your vest fabrics to suggest the four seasons of the year, for reversible fashions that are right for any time. Turn the treasure pouch inside out to match or contrast with the vests.

Materials and Tools

▶ Simple vest pattern, preferably one without darts

▶ Four different fabrics, 1 yd (.95 m) of each

▶ 1 yd (.95 m) cording for pouch

▶ Neutral color of thread for all fabrics

▶ Notions required by pattern

Instructions for Vests

1. Cut vest pattern out of all four fabrics.

2. Pair the fabrics for the inside and outside of each vest

3. With right sides together, sew shoulder seams of all inner and outer vests.

4. With right sides together, sew inner to outer vests along neckline, front opening, armhole, and hem edges. Do not sew side seams.

5. Turn vests right side out, pulling through the side openings. See Figure 1. Press both vests flat.

6. With right sides together, pin back

to front of outer vest at side seam. Sew along seamline, continuing stitching onto inner vest 1" (2.5 cm) beyond armhole and hemline seams. See Figure 2. Carefully press stitched seam open, keeping remaining unstitched portion of seam free. Turn vest right side out.

7. Turn under unstitched seam allowance of inner vest side seam; blind stitch in place.

Instructions for Pouch

1. Using scraps of two vest fabrics, cut two rectangles from each, to the desired finished pouch size plus ½" (1.25 cm) seam allowance.

2. With right sides together, sew two of the matching rectangles around three sides, leaving open at the top; turn pouch right side out and press flat.

3. Turn seam allowance of unstitched end to inside of pouch and press.

4. With right sides together, sew remaining two rectangles around three sides, leaving open at the top; do not turn second pouch right side out.

5. Turn down seam allowance of unstitched end and press; turned-down allowance is on outside or wrong side of pouch.

6. Slip second pouch inside first pouch, matching side seams.

7. Cut cording to a length that will be comfortable hanging around your neck, allowing ½" (1.25 cm) extra at each end.

8. Slip ends of cording between two pouches at side seams; topstitch two rows around pouch opening, being sure that cord ends are caught in stitching.

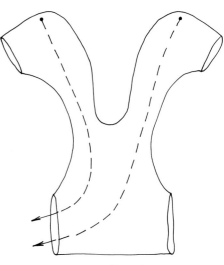

Figure 1
Turning vest through side seam

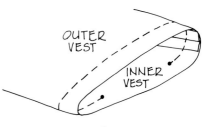

Figure 2
Stitching outer vest side seam and 1"(2.5cm)
beyond armhole and hem seams onto inner vest

▶ Add a simple flap to the pouch by inserting the stitched and turned flap shape in between the two pouches before topstitching, or by topstitching the flap to the outside back of the pouch.

▶ Make two pouches, one a bit smaller than the other, to slip inside the other for an extra safe hideaway.

SOPHISTICATED REVERSIBLE

Designed by M. Luanne Carson

A dressy black wool jacket is a favorite travel companion, but this reversible style is so much more. It combines the classic look with extra special buttons and an interesting rayon print for the alternate version.

Construction Notes From the Designer

▶ I selected a jacket pattern designed for a thick fabric like fleece, but used moderately thin fashion fabrics instead. The pattern therefore included enough ease to accommodate the double layers, so that the finished garment wouldn't be too small or tight. With a more closely fitted pattern, I would have cut one size larger than usual, to allow enough room for the multiple layers.

▶ I made the wool and rayon jackets separately. Then I placed one inside the other and bound the outer edges. This is quick and easy construction, and it also eliminates the uncomfortable bulk of many-layered seams.

▶ It's a bit tricky to get the layers to lie flat, so fabric choice is important. All layers, including internal fabrics, such as interfacing and underlining, should be able to slide against each other and not cling too much. When the jacket is turned to the other side, the layers should be able to shift a bit and hang without taut lines or ripples of excess fabric.

▶ To balance fabric layers in the pocket areas, I placed one pocket on the right-hand side of each jacket front. Regardless of which side shows, the jacket has a right-hand pocket on the outside and a left-hand pocket on the inside.

▶ I made buttonholes back-to-back in each jacket layer on both right and left fronts. Then I connected the buttons for each jacket to each other with thread shanks instead of sewing them directly to the fabric. The "two-headed" buttons can be slipped in and out of the buttonholes easily, depending on which buttons I want to wear with which jacket. This also makes it really easy to remove buttons when the jacket needs cleaning.

These "two-headed" shank buttons are easily removed when the jacket needs cleaning and they are just as reversible as the garment is. A dressy braid covers raw edges and adds a nice touch of contrast.

"In just a few short months, I traveled with this jacket from New York, to San Francisco, to Indiana. The temperatures ranged from the 30s to the 70s, but I was comfortable everywhere. The loose fit and drapey fabrics I chose for the two layers (wool crepe and rayon print) made it easy to push the sleeves up in warmer weather."

Have Vest Will Travel

Designed by Cathy Ham

Reversible vests are the perfect travel companions. They provide two totally different looks, can reverse from dressy to casual, are lightweight in the suitcase, and they attractively layer over other garments.

Materials and Tools

▶ Pattern for dartless vest
▶ Two different fabrics of choice, to yardage required by pattern
▶ Decorative buttons, trims, and other embellishments, as desired
▶ Notions required by pattern

Instructions For Basic Reversible Vest

1. Cut out pattern from both fabrics. You will make two separate vests, which are then sewn together to form a fully reversible garment.

2. Complete all pockets, pocket flaps, design details, and embellishments on each vest before sewing together.

3. Join shoulder seams on each vest and press open.

4. Place vests right sides together, carefully matching shoulder seams. Pin around armhole edges, front opening edges, and across bottom edges of fronts to about 3" (7.5 cm) from side seams. See illustration. Stitch all pinned edges, clip curves, and trim seam allowances.

5. Turn vest right side out through the shoulders. Press stitched edges.

6. Match underarm seams carefully, right sides together, and stitch front to back at side seams. Press seams open.

7. Close the bottom of the vest by stitching from the open section of the front bottoms across the side seams on either side, leaving about 6" (15 cm) open across bottom edge of vest back.

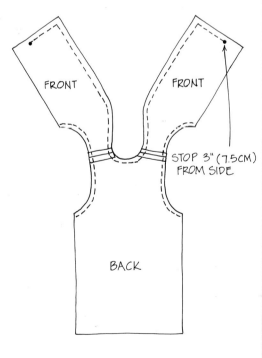

FRONT   FRONT

STOP 3" (7.5CM) FROM SIDE

BACK

"In one four-month peri-od, I traveled from Hong Kong to South Africa and several other far-away places. My favorite travel garments included a coat with two button-in linings (wool and cot-ton), and a bevy of easy-to-pack reversible vests. A few lightweight vests turned a basic dress into a whole wardrobe."

8. Turn vest right side out completely. Press remaining seam allowances under and neatly hand stitch opening closed.

9. If desired, topstitch armhole and outer edges. Complete any details, such as closures and buttons.

Designer *Tips*

▶ Pockets are practical and can also make a nice embellishment. Hide smaller pockets inside larger pockets, for keys, tickets, and other small valuables. Pocket flaps are great candidates for all manner of embellishments and they protect the contents of your pockets. Try using contrasting fabrics for pocket flaps or cover them completely with colorful buttons.

▶ Closures can also be decorative, from tabs and buckles to loops and braided cords. Just remember to stitch the ends of loops and cords into the seam when attaching the two vests. For a casual look, separating zippers can provide colorful contrast; they can also be decorated with snappy zipper pulls simply by adding interesting dangles to the hole in the zipper tab.

A pretty little appliqué design at one hip is a special and surprising touch of color to this denim vest.

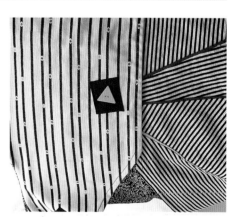

Colorful piping and a bright button sewn on top of an appliqué square of black fabric enhances the graphic design of this vest.

VEST WITH REVERSIBLE CAPELETS

Designed by Sonia A. Huber

This imaginative fashion combines a dressy vest with button-on reversible capelets to create a versatile garment that has several different looks.

Materials and Tools

▶ Vest pattern of choice
▶ Fabric of choice, as required by pattern, plus 1 yd (.95 m) for capelets
▶ Vest lining fabric of choice, as required by pattern
▶ 1 yd (.95) fabric of choice for reverse side of capelets
▶ Shoulder pads for vest
▶ Decorative buttons of choice
▶ Measuring and marking tools, including pencil and string
▶ Muslin or pattern-making paper, 45" (115 cm) wide
▶ Notions required by pattern

Instructions

1. Complete vest according to pattern instructions, inserting shoulder pads between vest fabric and lining. Shoulder pads are needed to support the weight of the capelets, without disrupting the hang of the vest. You also may want to stabilize the armhole edge of the vest with interfacing, to support the buttons.

2. Use the vest front and back pattern pieces to draft the capelet pattern, as follows. Overlap front and back pattern pieces along shoulder seamline; measure 1" (2.5 cm) in from armhole seamline and make a mark. See Figure 1. Measure from this mark straight down to the bottom of the armhole on both front and back, and note measurement. The vest shown here measures 8" (20.5 cm) from shoulder line to bottom of armhole.

3. Determine desired length of capelets by measuring from a point 1" (2.5 cm) above your shoulder point to your wrist. The vest shown here measures 25" (63.5 cm) to capelet hem.

4. Open out muslin and lay on flat surface. Make a mark along the fold-line to represent the shoulder mark on the pattern pieces. See Figure 2.

5. Measure straight down from this mark along the foldline to the desired capelet length and make another mark.

6. Tie a length of string to pencil; with pencil tip on the lower mark and end of the string at the upper mark, pivot the pencil to outer edges of muslin to make an evenly curved hemline.

7. Measure from upper mark out toward each side the armhole depth you measured in Step 2, and make a mark. Connect each mark to the outer edges of curved hemline with a straight line. This is the capelet

working pattern; from this point, you will work with the muslin on a dress form or a friend's body.

8. Cut out the capelet muslin and pin in place at the shoulder. Begin folding back the front and back edges of the muslin until you identify a pleasant drape and the top edge of the capelet hangs straight from front to back. Mark the fold-back lines on the muslin and trim away the excess; this is your finished capelet pattern. See Figure 3.

9. Cut the pattern out of both capelet fabrics, adding seam allowances to all four sides.

10. If embellishing the capelets with decorative embroidery, braid, or embellishment, do it now.

11. Stabilize the top edge of capelet with an interfacing strip.

12. With right sides together, stitch both sets of capelets together along side and bottom edges. Trim seam allowances, turn to right side through unstitched top edge, and press.

13. Bind the raw top edge of each capelet with bias binding, grosgrain ribbon, leather strip, or other desired material.

14. Pin finished capelet to finished vest at shoulder and adjust for an attractive drape. Determine number of buttonholes required to hold capelet in place and mark location 1" (2.5 cm) in from armhole edge.

15. Make buttonholes in bound edge of capelets; sew buttons to vest.

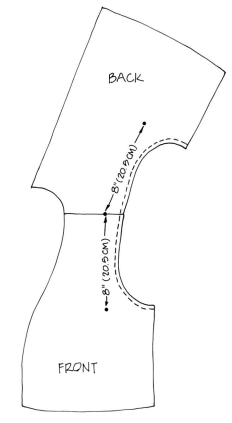

BACK

8" (20.5 CM)

8" (20.5 CM)

FRONT

Figure 1

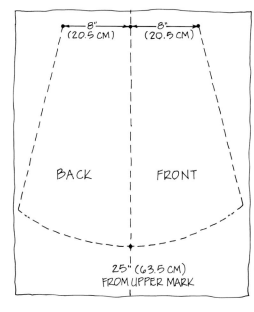

8" (20.5 CM)   8" (20.5 CM)

BACK   FRONT

25" (63.5 CM) FROM UPPER MARK

Figure 2

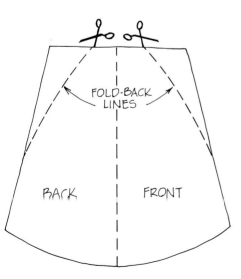

FOLD-BACK
LINES

BACK   FRONT

Figure 3

Designer Tips

▶ When selecting fabrics for the capelets, remember that sheers and radically different colors may "shadow" through to the other side. But don't rule them out; you can get some nice reversible effects by layering a sheer or lacy fabric over a print or solid.

▶ To be sure the capelets will reverse correctly, make sure all the buttons and buttonhole sizes are the same. If you do use different sizes, you'll have to reverse the capelets and swap them to the other shoulder to match up buttons and buttonholes.

Custom Coordinate Jacket

Designed by Caryl Rae Hancock

Pull an entire travel wardrobe together with this custom jacket that goes with every other item you pack, is a comfortable all-climate garment, and will be a perfect finishing touch for any occasion.

Materials and Tools

▸ Pattern for simple, untailored jacket

▸ Assorted scraps from other garments in your travel wardrobe and/or your fabric stash. You will need approximately 30 percent more fabric than the pattern calls for. For example, if the jacket pattern calls for 3 yds (3.75 m), the fabric scraps will need to total at least 4 yds (3.7 m), to allow for waste.

▸ Approximately $\frac{5}{8}$ yd (.6 m) cotton knit ribbing in coordinating color, for finishing front opening, hem, and sleeves. If you lengthen the jacket pattern, remember to purchase extra ribbing.

▸ Fusible interfacing in weight appropriate for selected fabrics

▸ Marking and cutting tools, or rotary cutter and mat

▸ Notions required by pattern

Instructions

1. Interface fabrics as needed for stability and to equalize overall weight of jacket.

2. Lay out jacket back pattern piece and measure at its widest point; add 2-4" (5-10 cm) to arrive at a number easily divided by 3, and then divide by 3. For example, if the widest point of the back pattern piece measures 27" (68.5 cm), add 3" (7.5 cm) to equal 30" (76 cm); then divide by 3 to arrive at 10" (25.5 cm). You will cut the scraps of fabric into 10" (25.5 cm) widths and assorted lengths, to get three strips of pieced fabric for the jacket back. See Figure 1.

3. Repeat for left and right jacket fronts, and two sleeves.

4. Cut assorted fabrics to the width you just determined and in varying lengths, from 2-8" (5-20.5 cm).

5. Begin stitching cut pieces to one another, right sides together. Insert fringe, strips of folded fabric, or decorative trim into the seams, as desired. Vary colors, design motifs, and textures for interest. Press seams in one direction. Continue piecing strips until you have enough to cover the jacket pattern pieces.

6. Lay out the strips on a flat surface and arrange them in a pleasing fashion. You may need to add an extra piece of fabric here or there, to offset the strips so that the same fabric doesn't end up next to itself.

7. When satisfied with the arrangement, stitch the three back strips together lengthwise, right sides together. Press seams to one side. Repeat with front and sleeve strips.

8. Cut out the jacket and assemble, according to pattern instructions.

9. Cut a piece of ribbing to desired width (when folded) and long enough for jacket hem. Fold in half lengthwise and stitch to bottom edge of jacket, stretching ribbing slightly to ease in the jacket hem. Trim any excess ribbing from center front edges. See Figure 2.

10. Cut two pieces of ribbing for front opening; stitch together at one short end. Fold ribbing in half, with stitched seam on the inside. Place ribbing seam at center back of neck, and pin ribbing to jacket, right sides together, from back of neck to a point 12" (30.5 cm) from bottom edge.

11. Beginning at back of neck, stitch ribbing to jacket opening, stopping about 12" (30.5 cm) from bottom edge.

12. Determine remaining ribbing length required to finish front edge to bottom of hem ribbing; trim off excess. Fold unsewn ribbing in half, right sides together, and stitch end.

"I spent a month in the Far East with my husband, on a trip that included casual sightseeing and formal receptions. As a confirmed fabric-aholic, I wanted to take a versatile wardrobe, but a minimum of individual garments. This would leave me more room in the suitcase to bring home new fabrics. So I designed and sewed a basic wardrobe of interchangeable blouses, slacks, and skirts. Then I made this one jacket to go with all of them, using fabric scraps from the travel garments and other clothes I've made."

13. Turn right side out and finish stitching ribbing to front edge of jacket. See Figure 3.

14. For sleeve ribbing, measure wrist and add about 1½" (4 cm), for ease and seam allowance. Cut two pieces of ribbing to this length and stitch the short ends together, to form a circle. Make sure your hand will comfortably fit through this circle.

15. Fold sleeve ribbing in half, matching raw edges and with seam on the inside. Stitch raw edges to end of jacket sleeves, stretching ribbing to fit, and matching ribbing seam to jacket underarm seam.

Designer Tips

❱ When selecting fabrics for this jacket, consider the care requirements of each one. If your entire travel wardrobe is cotton, use cottons for the jacket and you'll have a fully washable garment. However, if your wardrobe is a mix of different fabrics, plan to hand wash the jacket in cold water and hang it to dry.

❱ Strips of fabrics in your stash can be attractively unraveled and sewn into the seams, for a coordinating fringe.

❱ If you plan to serge all seams, think about using decorative threads in both loopers and then letting the seams show on the right side, for a creative alternative.

Figure 1
Measure jacket pattern pieces at widest point and divide by 3, to determine width of pieced strips.

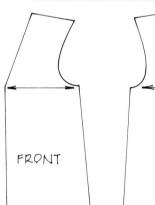

FRONT

BACK

SLEEVE

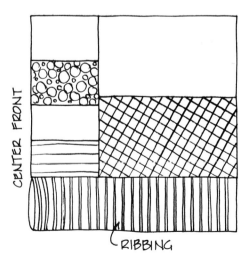

Figure 2   Hem Ribbing

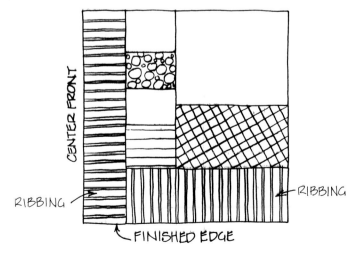

Figure 3   Front Ribbing

REVERSIBLE PUZZLE VEST

Designed by M. Luanne Carson

Express your creativity with this fun interweaving technique. Then use the resulting puzzle fabric as one layer of an artistic reversible fashion.

Materials and Tools

▶ Pattern for simple vest without darts or pleats

▶ Three coordinating fabrics, each in amount required by pattern

▶ Tailor's chalk

▶ Decorative buttons of choice

▶ Notions required by pattern

Construction Notes From the Designer

▶ Choose two fabrics for the interwoven vest layer; the third fabric will be the vest lining or reversible layer. It's helpful, and lots of fun, to experiment with scraps of different fabrics for the interweaving; many different effects are possible with pastels, high-contrast colors, prints, solids, and textures. To get comfortable with the over-under plain weave technique and various color interactions, practice with strips of colored paper before slashing any fabric.

▶ Before beginning the interweaving, cut rectangles out of all three fabrics that are a bit larger than the vest pattern pieces. Don't forget to cut

rectangles for both a right and left vest front, as well as a vest back.

▶ Start with one fabric rectangle and cut a series of vertical slashes from one edge to, but not through, its opposite edge. Cut the second fabric rectangle horizontally from one edge to, but not through, its opposite edge. You can cut straight strips of uniform size, or play around with curving or angular strips of varying sizes. Carefully place one set of strips on top of the other and begin to weave, one vertically-cut strip moving under a horizontally-cut strip and over the next. Continue this over one, under one, over one, under one weaving until all strips are woven. Repeat this process with the other vest fabric rectangles.

▶ Carefully pin the woven fabric rectangles on top of the lining fabric rectangles. Machine stitch all raw edges, through all layers, with a wide zigzag or decorative stitch. This holds the woven strips securely and gently quilts the vest. When stitching is completed, place the pattern pieces on their designated rectangles and use the tailor's chalk to trace the outline. Cut out the pieces and construct the vest, according to pattern instructions. Finish the outer and armhole edges with decorative braid or serge them with Woolly nylon thread in both loopers of the machine.

▶ Once you experiment with the weaving technique a few times, you'll be more confident about pre-planning certain visual effects like

the focal point on the back side of the vest shown here. But no matter how carefully you plan ahead, you're bound to be surprised by the results of the interlacing. Be sure to look at both sides of the weaving; you might be surprised by the "wrong" side and decide let it show instead.

▶ For a quick and easy fastener, make a button loop from edging braid or trim and then sew two buttons together back to back (one button on each side of the vest) through all layers. The loop easily slips over the button, regardless of which side is showing.

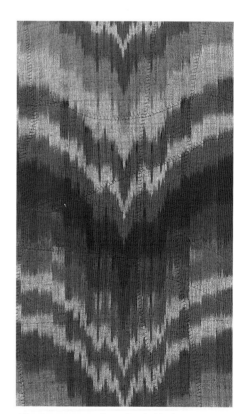

The decorative stitching that holds the strips together on the interwoven side also makes a nice design on this reverse or lining side.

REVERSIBLE SKIRT OVERLAY

Designed by Sonia A. Huber

This quick-sew reversible overlay is an easy way to multiply wardrobe options. Wear a coordinating reversible skirt by itself or with either side of this traveling companion.

Materials and Tools

▶ Skirt pattern of choice

▶ Two coordinating fabrics, each in the amount required by pattern

▶ Approximately 80" (2 m) cording or ribbon, for ties

▶ Tracing or pattern-making paper

▶ Measuring and marking tools

▶ Elastic for waistband

▶ Notions required by pattern

Instructions

1. Trace skirt front pattern piece, marking lines along actual waistline and actual hemline. Mark point A at center front of waistline, and point B at side waist cutting line. See illustration on next page.

2. Measure between point A and B; extend waistline beyond side cutting line by half the measured amount. Mark as point C.

3. At center front, measure up 6" (15 cm) from actual hemline and

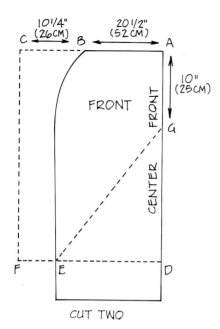

C ←10¼" (26CM)→ B ←20½" (52CM)→ A

FRONT

CENTER FRONT

10" (25CM)

G

F E D

CUT TWO

mark as point D. At side cutting line, measure up 6" (15 cm) from actual hemline and mark as point E.

4. Draw a line from point D through point E, to a length that equals A-C. Mark the stopping point as F. Connect points C and F with a straight line.

5. At center front, measure down 10" (25.5 cm) from point A and mark as point G. Connect points G and E with a straight line.

6. Add seam allowances to these lines: A-C, F-E, E-G, G-A. NOTE: The seam allowance is already included in line C-F.

7. Place skirt back pattern piece under tracing paper with the paper's edge aligned with center back fold-line or center back cutting line. Trace actual waistline and actual hemline. Mark point A at center back foldline or cutting line, and point B at side waist cutting line.

8. Mark points C, D, E, and F, and draw lines as you did on the front.

9. Add seam allowances to these lines: A-C, D-F. NOTE: The seam allowance is already included in line C-F.

10. Cut newly drafted front and back pattern pieces from both fabrics.

11. Sew fronts to backs at side seams on both overlays.

12. With right sides together, sew two overlays together along hemline and front opening edge; press and turn right side out.

13. Measure and cut waistband to fit your waist, plus seam allowances at each end, minus the amount desired for front separation. You can make a single-color waistband that looks well with either side, or a two-color band that matches each side of the overlay fabric.

14. Cut elastic to equal waistband, minus 3" (7.5 cm).

15. Cut four cord or ribbon ties about 20" (51 cm) long, or make matching bias cord from overlay fabric. Knot one end of each tie.

16. Insert elastic and attach waistband to overlay, catching unknotted ends of cord ties and ends of elastic into stitching at each end of band.

Designer Tip

▶ This elastic-waist overlay is perfect for lots of traveling, especially if you eat well along the way. The slightly elastic waist flexes with your figure, and the front opening can draw closer together or spread further apart without changing the attractive look.

TROPICAL PAINTED VEST
Designed by Anne McCloskey

Once you get back home, make a vest and then paint a memento of the landscape you saw during your travels. This technique is fast and easy.

Materials and Tools

▶ Store-bought or finished vest, made from natural fibers, preferably with large surface areas to paint on

▶ Fabric paints in assorted colors

▶ Assorted brushes with round and square tips

▶ Black permanent markers, fine- and medium-line

▶ Transfer paper and pencil

▶ Newspaper

Instructions

1. Draw or photocopy designs that you remember from your travel adventures. The vest shown here reminds the designer of the tropical flowers and bright colors of a Caribbean vacation.

2. If using a store-bought vest, wash and iron it to remove sizing.

3. Review paint directions. Experiment with markers, brushes, and paints on paper and/or fabric scraps to determine different paint strokes and brush effects. For example, try a swirling motion with the brush as well as a staccato dabbing

motion. Mix colors as desired, lighten colors with a bit of additional water, or paint one color on top of another for different color-blending effects.

4. With front side facing up, line inside of vest with several layers of newspaper, to prevent paint from seeping through to back.

5. Determine placement of designs and transfer design outlines to vest front.

6. Begin painting design, using square-tip brush for larger areas of color and round-tip brush for smaller, more detailed areas.

7. When finished, allow paint to dry, and then outline parts of the design as desired with a permanent marker. Don't outline every motif or shape, because the overall design will appear too dark.

8. When completely dry, remove newspaper, and repeat on back side of vest.

9. If paint directions call for heat-setting, use a pressing cloth. Do not touch painted areas directly with the iron.

REVERSIBLE BLOUSE AND WRAP SKIRT

Designed by Mary Russell

*F*or *two quick and casual outfits, make a simple wrap skirt in a reversible version and a coordinated pullover to go with either side.*

Construction Notes From the Designer

▶ Any uncomplicated pattern can be easily made up for reversible wear. Just be sure to select fabrics that are compatible in weight, drape, and method of care. I find rayons are a good choice because they are lightweight, comfortable to wear in most climates, and they don't wrinkle too easily.

▶ If you choose a solid for one side and a pattern for the other, you get many wearing possibilities. You can wear the solid by itself or with your creatively patchworked vest or jacket, and you can also mix and match the solid and patterned sides.

▶ On a reversible skirt, press the darts toward the side seams on one layer and toward the center on the other. This ensures that the skirt will pack flat and not be bulky to wear.

▶ To further reduce bulk, I don't bother with buttons on both sides of the skirt. When I wear the print side out, the buttons show, but when I reverse the skirt, it buttons invisibly on the inside.

EASY REVERSIBLE VEST

Designed by Pat Scheible

*A*dd *a lightweight layer of warmth over a basic dress for attractive business wear or a cozy evening look.*

Construction Notes From the Designer

▶ Given a piece of fabric with two equally attractive sides, what do you do? Make a reversible garment! I chose a simple vest pattern and made it with flat felled seams, instead of lining it. Then I stitched piping to the seamline along the outer edges (neckline, front opening, armhole, and hemline), and turned the seam allowance under (see illustration). To hide the seam allowance, I simply stitched a coordinating flat braid on top of the raw edge. The braid is visible only on one side, but the vest still looks good on either side.

The flat braid adds an extra bit of color to this otherwise plain side, but it also hides the raw edge of the seam allowance.

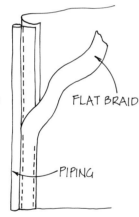

FLAT BRAID

PIPING

▶ I added a button loop and wonderful antique button to one side. When wearing the other side out, I just let the vest hang open for a more casual look.

NYLON TOTE BAG

Designed by Lisa Sanders

This efficient tote is good-looking, lightweight, and washable. It also expands to accommodate the treasures you find along the way.

Materials and Tools

▶ 1 yd (.95 m) nylon fabric

▶ 18" (45.5 cm) heavy-duty nylon zipper

▶ Ruler

▶ Thread to match

▶ Piece of heavy cardboard, 3" by 15" (7.5 by 38 cm)

Instructions

1. Cut the fabric into the following pieces:

—two rectangles for bag front and back, 20" by 13" (51 by 33 cm)

—one rectangle for pocket, 20" by 9" (51 by 23 cm)

—one rectangle for base, 16" by 4" (40.5 by 10 cm)

—one rectangle for top zipper band, 37" by 5" (94 by 12.5 cm)

—two strips for handles, 28" by 2" (71 by 5 cm)

2. Turn top edge of pocket piece under ⅜" (1 cm); turn under again ⅜" (1 cm) and stitch ¼" (6 mm) from fold. Position pocket on bag front, matching side and bottom edges; baste in place.

3. Fold pocket/front in half to mark center dividing line of pocket. Stitch pocket division along crease, starting at bottom edge and sewing straight up to top edge, backstitching at top edge to reinforce.

4. With right sides together, sew bag front to back at side seams; finish seam allowances with serger or zigzag stitch.

5. With right sides together, sew one bag base piece to front/back, pivoting at corners. Clip corners on front/back. See Figure 1.

6. Lay other bag base piece on top of first base piece, and stitch to seam allowance. Finish all seam allowances with serger or zigzag stitch. Turn bag right side out.

7. To make handles, fold strips in half lengthwise and stitch ¼" (6 mm) from long edge. Turn right side out and press. Topstitch each long edge ¼" (6 mm) from edge.

8. Position handles 5½" (14 cm) in from side seams and stitch ends securely to top edge. See Figure 2.

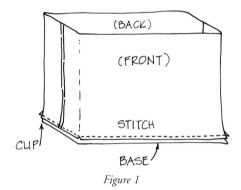

Figure 1

▶ The cardboard piece stiffens the bottom and helps the bag hold its shape. Remove it whenever the bag needs laundering. However, if the bag won't be washable, you can slip the cardboard between the two base pieces before stitching.

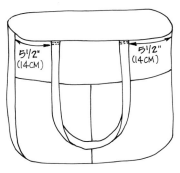

Figure 2

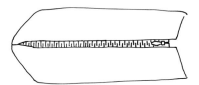

Figure 3

Figure 4

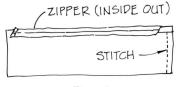

Figure 5

9. With right sides together, fold top zipper band piece in half, matching 5" (12.5 cm) edges; stitch from folded edge along seamline for 1" (2.5 cm) and backstitch securely. See Figure 3.

10. Lightly press remaining seam open and insert zipper. See Figure 4.

11. With right sides together, stitch remaining 5" (12.5 cm) edge closed. See Figure 5.

12. With right sides together, stitch top zipper band to top edge of bag front/back. Open zipper to make this step easier. See Figure 6.

13. Turn bag right side out, push zipper band down to inside of bag and handles to outside. Edgestitch very close to top edge of bag, through zipper band and handle ends; repeat ¼" (6 mm) from edge. This helps zip-

per band stay hidden inside bag, unless you pull it out to accommodate a larger load.

14. Insert cardboard into base of bag.

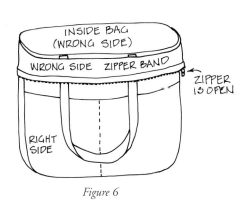

Figure 6

POCKET ON A STRING

Designed by Jane Benton Butler

This handy tote for personal or business items is a small, yet convenient, travel companion and it doubles as a creative fashion accessory.

Materials and Tools

NOTE: Finished size of tote shown here is 6" x 8½" (15 x 21.5 cm) with 42" (106.5 cm) strap.

▶ Tapestry or upholstery fabric, or faux leather for outer bag: 6" x 17" (15 x 43 cm)

▶ ½ yd (.5 m) lining fabric

▶ Assorted scraps of Ultrasuede in coordinating colors

▶ 1½ yd (1.4 m) cording for strap

▶ Fusible web product (optional)

▶ Thread to match fabric

▶ Assorted embellishments

"When I travel for work, I often find myself in a trade show booth or navigating a professional conference. I don't want to be loaded down with a full-sized purse, but I must be able to carry a hotel key, pen, business cards, credit cards, eyeglasses, and a bit of cash. Women's business garments rarely have adequate pockets for these items, so this tote functions as a decorative exterior pocket and a stylish accessory at the same time."

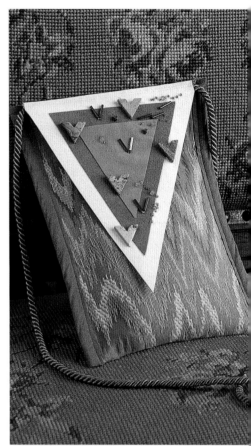

Designer Tips

▶ I cut triangle-shaped the business card pockets to coordinate with the sharp angles in the tapestry pattern, but let your fabric speak to you!

▶ Put the business card pockets on the outside of the tote for easiest access. Other items that need a bit more protection can be safely hidden inside.

Instructions

1. Cut lining pieces as follows:
—one piece 6" x 17" (15 x 43 cm), for tote lining
—one piece 7" x 4" (18 x 10 cm), for inside eyeglass pocket
—two pieces 4¾ x 3½" (12 x 9 cm), for small inside pockets

2. On each pocket piece, fold edges under ¼" (6 mm), and then another ¼" (6 mm) all around; top-stitch one short end (this will be the top edge of the inside pockets).

3. Arrange pocket pieces as desired on lining; topstitch in place close to side and bottom edges.

4. Cut outer business card pockets in desired shapes from Ultrasuede scraps and topstitch where desired at one end of tapestry fabric.

5. To make flap, use fusible web to bond two layers of lightweight Ultrasuede together and cut out desired flap shape. Stitch flap securely to end of tapestry fabric and embellish as desired with fabric scraps, beads, or embroidery.

6. Butt ends of cording underneath flap, and hand stitch cording in place across width of tote.

7. With right sides together, stitch one end of lining to one end of tapestry fabric; turn right side out. Narrow hem other end of lining.

8. Fold up front of bag to outside, matching side edges; tack lining hem in place at other end of tapestry fabric. Bind side edges with Ultrasuede.

HANDS-FREE BELT POUCH
Designed by Susan Hart Henegar

*F*ree up your hands with this quick-to-make pouch that slips on a belt and makes the perfect carrier for camera, travel journal, or assorted necessaries.

Materials and Tools

▶ 2-2½ sq ft (61-76 sq cm) soft leather or canvas

▶ ⅜ yd (.35 m) lining fabric (optional)

▶ One twist toggle closure

▶ Fusible web product

▶ Measuring and marking tools

▶ Sewing machine needle appropriate for leather, size 18 or 20

▶ Heavy duty quilting or nylon thread

"Because of the usual stresses of commercial sewing and weaving, as well as a whiplash accident several years ago, I am extremely careful about the weight of the bags I carry on my shoulder. I stitched my first belt pouch from scraps left from a leather jacket on the evening before an overseas trip. I knew I would be carrying a small camera, notebook, and snack, and I didn't want to fuss with a purse each day. This simple pouch is easy to get in and out of, but it sticks close to your body."

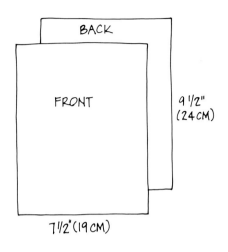

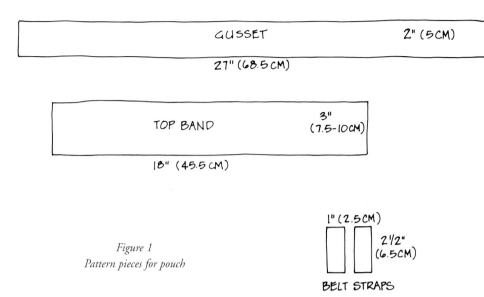

Figure 1
Pattern pieces for pouch

Instructions

NOTE: Finished size of the pouch shown here is 9" x 7" (23 x 18 cm).

1. Determine desired finished size of your pouch, and cut the front and back pieces, gusset, belt straps, and top band from desired fabric as shown in Figure 1. Allow scant 1/4" (6 mm) seam allowances, to minimize wasted leather.

2. Cut same pieces from lining fabric, if desired.

3. Sew belt straps to back side of pouch.

4. Sew one long edge of gusset to side and bottom edges of front in 1/4" (6 mm) seams; sew other long edge to back.

5. Repeat for lining, stitching slightly wider seams so lining will fit inside pouch.

6. Slip lining inside pouch, matching up seamlines. Set the "male" part of the toggle on the inside back, near the top of the pouch. If necessary, use fusible web to stabilize lining and leather, and keep the two layers aligned.

7. Fold the top band in half lengthwise; wrap over top edge of pouch and topstitch close to edge of band, trimming band to fit around "male" toggle part. Be sure the band covers the back side of the male toggle part.

8. Set the "female" part of the toggle on the front of the pouch.

ON-THE-GO BACKPACK

Designed by Char TerBeest-Kudla

This good-looking backpack features high style as well as efficient storage space. Interesting fabrics make it uniquely yours.

Materials and Tools

▶ Upholstery or heavy-weight fabric: ½ yd (.5 m) for body of pack; ½ yd (.5 m) for flap and bottom of pack; ¼ yd (.25 m) for pocket

▶ Cotton blend or other lining fabric: ½ yd (.5 m) for body of pack; ½ yd (.5 m) for flap and inside pocket

▶ Heavyweight interfacing: 2" by 3" (5 by 7.5 cm)

▶ Nylon zippers: 7" (18 cm) for flap; 16" (40.5 cm) for front pocket

▶ Poly webbing, 1" (2.5 cm) wide: one 12" (30.5 cm) length for hanging loop at top of bag; two 6" (15 cm) lengths for front buckle

▶ Poly webbing, 1½" (4 cm) wide: two 6" (15 cm) lengths for back oval rings; two 44" (112 cm) or greater lengths for shoulder straps

▶ One 1" (2.5 cm) side-squeeze buckle to join flap to bag

▶ Two 1½" (4 cm) oval rings for shoulder straps

- Two 1½" (4 cm) slip-through or ladder locks for shoulder straps
- Two sets grommets for bag draw string
- One locking toggle for drawstring
- Round shoe string or cord, 42" (106.5 cm) long
- Rattail cording, 12" (30.5 cm) long
- Thread appropriate for selected fabric
- Two charms for embellishing rattail cord on pocket zipper (optional)

Instructions

NOTE: Seam allowances are ⅝" (1.5 cm).

1. Measure and cut all fabric and lining rectangles, according to cutting diagram on page 100.

2. Shape and cut out all flap and bottom pieces, according to cutting diagram.

Front Flap:

1. Pin flap linings to wrong side of flaps. Set one lining/flap piece aside.

2. On other piece, measure and mark a line 2¾" (7 cm) up from the wider center front end; cut along

line. See Figure 1. Serge or zigzag each side of cut.

3. Separate side-squeeze buckle. Loop one 6" (15 cm) length of 1" (2.5 cm) webbing through top half of buckle, matching raw ends; baste webbing to split flap section at center front, with buckle end toward curved edge and webbing ends toward straight edge.

4. Satin stitch or zigzag 7" (18 cm) zipper tapes together above zipper pull and below zipper stop.

5. Stitch zipper to cut edge of larger flap section, then to smaller flap section, catching basted webbing ends in the seam.

6. Turn webbing down and stitch to right side of lower flap to hold buckle in place.

7. With right sides together, stitch lined flap pieces together, leaving narrow end (at center back) unstitched. Turn and press; baste unstitched end closed. During remaining construction, remember that the zipper side of the front flap is the right side and faces out.

Front Pocket:

1. Measure and mark a line on front pocket piece 2" (5 cm) from one long edge; cut along line. Serge or zigzag each side of cut.

2. Satin stitch or zigzag 16" (40.5 cm) zipper tapes together above zipper pull; shorten zipper to fit cut edge of front pocket and carefully

zigzag across lower zipper teeth by hand or machine.

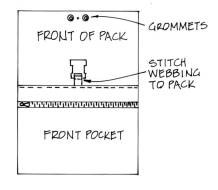

Figure 2

3. Stitch zipper to cut edges of front pocket as you did with flap pocket. See Figure 2.

4. Press under ½" (1.25 cm) along long edge above pocket zipper.

5. Pin pocket to right side of one backpack body piece, with bottom edges even; baste along side and bottom edges.

6. Loop remaining 6" (15 cm) length of 1" (2.5 cm) webbing through bottom half of side-squeeze buckle, matching raw ends; slip webbing ends between pack body and folded top edge of pocket; baste at center front, leaving 1" (2.5 cm) of webbing exposed above fold. Buckle should point up toward top of bag.

7. Stitch folded top edge of pocket to pack body, catching webbing in seam.

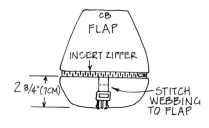

Figure 1

8. Stitch exposed webbing to right side of pack body to hold buckle in place.

Backpack Body:

1. Fold under ¼" (6 mm) along all sides of inside pocket; edgestitch along one edge of pocket (this will be the top edge or pocket opening). Position pocket where desired on one backpack lining piece, with stitched edge on top; stitch pocket in place along side and bottom edges. Set aside.

2. Loop two 6" (15 cm) lengths of 1½" (4 cm) webbing through oval rings, matching raw ends. Baste webbing ends to bottom edge of remaining pack body piece (without

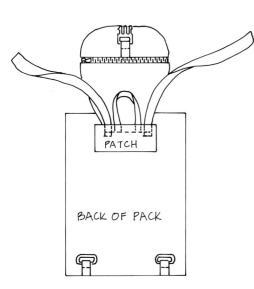

Figure 3

pocket) approximately 3" (7.5 cm) from each side edge; ends with oval rings should point toward top of bag. Stitch webbing down to body to hold oval rings in place. See Figure 3.

3. Position basted end of flap in cen-

ter of pack body piece at end opposite the oval rings, several inches from top edge and pin in place; zipper end of flap should extend beyond top edge of back body.

4. Fold 12" (30.5 cm) length of webbing into a "U" shape, for the hanging loop, and position at middle of flap, matching raw ends of webbing to raw edge of flap; baste in place. Hanging loop should point toward zipper end of flap.

5. Position two 44" (112 cm) lengths

of webbing at outer edges of flap, on either side of hanging loop, with raw ends of webbing at least 1" (2.5 cm) below raw edge of flap.

6. Stitch flap and webbing securely to pack body; use small straight or zigzag stitches and as many rows of stitching as desired.

7. To cover raw edges and stitching, make a patch of coordinating fabric cut large enough to cover flap and ends of webbing straps. Press under edges of patch and topstitch to pack body.

8. Pin lining piece with inside pocket to wrong side of this pack body piece, and set aside.

Backpack Body Assembly:

1. On pack body piece with zippered front pocket, measure and mark a center point 1½" (4 cm) from top edge. Pin interfacing to wrong side of fabric at this point; this will reinforce the grommets.

2. Pin remaining lining piece to wrong side of fabric.

3. Apply grommets on either side of marked point, ½" (1.25 cm) apart. See Figure 2.

4. With right sides together, stitch pack body pieces together along side edges, keeping webbing straps free. Serge or zigzag seam allowances to clean finish.

5. Baste pack bottom pieces together, wrong sides together.

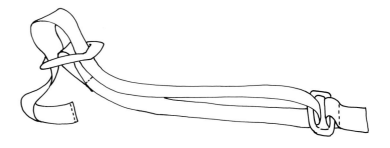

Figure 4

6. Pin pack bottom to right side of pack body, easing bottom to fit, and trimming excess from bottom if needed. Stitch, and serge or zigzag seam allowance to clean finish; turn pack right side out.

Finishing:

1. To form drawstring casing, turn under top of edge pack ¾" (2 cm), and again 1" (2.5 cm); stitch close to bottom fold.

2. Pull drawstring cord through casing. Insert cord ends through locking toggle, and tie ends into knot.

3. Insert webbing straps through slip-through locks, oval rings, and back through slip-through locks. Melt ends of webbing and stitch down to itself. See Figure 4.

4. Lace rattail cord through zipper pull on front pocket; tie a knot to secure and embellish cord ends with optional charms.

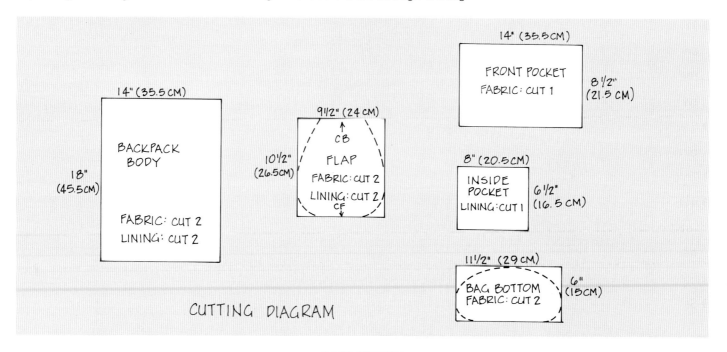

14" (35.5 CM)

FRONT POCKET
FABRIC: CUT 1

8 ½"
(21.5 CM)

14" (35.5 CM)

BACKPACK BODY

18"
(45.5 CM)

FABRIC: CUT 2
LINING: CUT 2

9½" (24 CM)

CB

FLAP
FABRIC: CUT 2
LINING: CUT 2
CF

10½"
(26.5 CM)

8" (20.5 CM)

INSIDE POCKET
LINING: CUT 1

6½"
(16.5 CM)

11½" (29 CM)

BAG BOTTOM
FABRIC: CUT 2

6"
(15 CM)

CUTTING DIAGRAM

TRAVELING PROFESSIONAL'S TOTE

Designed by Jane Benton Butler

*T*his handsome bag is a hard-working traveler's tote, with one interior division for reading materials and several pockets for personal items.

Materials and Tools

NOTE: Finished size of tote shown here is 15" x 16" (38.5 x 40.5 cm) and 4½" (11.5 cm) deep.

▶ Fabric for outer bag: 1⅛ yd (1.1 m) of 45" (115 cm) fabric or 1 yd (.95m) of 60" (152 cm) fabric. The designer chose polyester microfiber for the bag shown here.

▶ 2 yds (1.85 m) of 21" (53.5 cm) fusible interfacing

▶ ½ yd (.5 m) fabric for inner divider and pockets. The designer recommends a sturdy fabric such as rayon twill lining or heavyweight cotton.

▶ 3 yds (2.75 m) of 1" (2.5 cm) webbing for straps

▶ Thread to match outer fabric

▶ 4½" x 15" (11.5 x 38 cm) rectangle of stiff plastic mesh, such as needlepoint mesh, for base

▶ Fray retardant

▶ Set of four metal purse feet (optional)

"I travel a lot for business, mostly by air, and need to control all my 'stuff.' I always use a tote bag to carry newspaper and other reading material, snacks, jewelry that I don't want to pack in checked luggage, prescription medicines, airline tickets, passport, hand lotion, small cosmetic bag, and wallet. This tote fits under the seat, keeps everything together, and is easy to carry in case I also must haul a laptop computer."

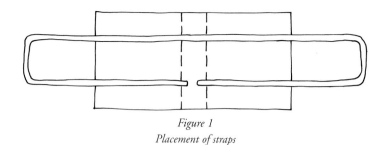

Figure 1
Placement of straps

Instructions

NOTE: Seam allowances are ½" (1.25 cm) unless otherwise noted.

1. For outer bag, cut fabric and interfacing as follows:

—one main piece 16" x 38" (40.5 x 96.5 cm)

—two side pieces 17" x 6" (43 x 15 cm)

2. Fuse interfacing to wrong side of each piece, according to manufacturer's directions. Finish all edges with overlock stitch.

3. Fold under ½" (1.25 cm) along both ends of main piece and one narrow end of side pieces; topstitch. These will be the top edges of the finished tote.

4. Apply fray retardant to ends of webbing. Arrange webbing on main fabric piece 4" (10 cm) from each side, starting at center of bottom and continuing in a loop, being careful not to twist; pin in place. See Figure 1. Stitch over ends of webbing with a wide zigzag stitch.

5. Topstitch close to each edge of webbing, backstitching where straps extend beyond edges of fabric.

6. Cut divider piece 18" x 34" (45.5 x 86.5 cm) and interface one half. Divider piece is cut a little wider and eased to fit outer bag, to allow enough space to insert contents.

7. Fold divider piece in half, right sides together, to 18" x 17" (45.5 x 43 cm). Stitch around all edges, leaving an opening large enough to turn divider right side out; turn and slip stitch opening closed. Topstitch ½" (1.25 cm) from top edge.

8. Cut pocket piece 17" x 20" (43 x 51 cm) and interface one half.

9. Fold pocket piece in half, right sides together, to 17" x 10" (43 x 25.5 cm). Stitch, turn, and slip stitch opening as you did with the divider piece.

10. Apply pocket piece to divider 1" (2.5 cm) from top edge and ½" (1.25 cm) in from each side. See Figure 2.

11. Stitch pocket to divider in sections, as desired, arranging fabric ease to allow space for bulky items, such as eyeglasses. The designer subdivided this tote's pockets as follows:

—4" x 9" (10 x 23 cm) for airline tickets

—4" x 6" (10 x 15 cm) for passport

—1" x 6" (2.5 x 15 cm) for pen

—3" x 6" (7.5 x 15 cm) for glasses

—4" x 9" (10 x 23 cm) for miscellaneous papers in a #10 envelope

12. Pin divider to one end of outer fabric rectangle, being sure that pocket openings point toward top-stitched edge. Baste along sides and bottom, creating pleats at outer bottom corners of divider to take up excess fabric.

13. With right sides together, join side pieces to main piece, clipping main piece to pivot at corners. Tack corners into a fold if desired.

14. Cut a piece of divider fabric 7" x 18" (18 x 45.5 cm). Wrap around edges of plastic mesh, place in base of bag, and tack in place.

15. Apply metal purse feet if desired.

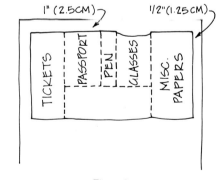

Figure 2
Stitching lines for pockets

FOLD-FLAT TRAVEL TOTE

Designed by Susan Hart Henegar

*W*ondering how to get those great travel purchases back home? This roomy satchel conveniently packs flat to fit inside other luggage, ready to carry a load when necessary.

Materials and Tools

▶ 1 yd (.95 m) rubberized vinyl, backed taffeta, canvas, or auto convertible top fabric

▶ 1⅜ yd (1.3 m) heavy duty zipper and two slides or pulls

▶ 1¼ yd (1.15 m) seatbelt strap or nylon webbing

▶ Four large commercial grade snaps for "feet" (optional)

▶ Measuring and marking tools

▶ Sewing machine needles appropriate for leather, size 18 or 20

▶ Heavy duty quilting or nylon thread

Instructions

NOTE: Folding tote shown here measures 12" x 16½" (30.5 x 42), to fit inside a 13" x 18" (33 x 45.5) suitcase when folded flat.

1. Choose a size that is about 1" (2.5 cm) smaller all around than the case you plan to pack this satchel into.

Lay out pattern like an envelope, to fit the selected fabric, along lengthwise or crosswise grain, adding ½" (1.25 cm) seam allowances. See Figure 1 on page 104.

2. Cut out of a single layer of fabric.

3. Mark position of optional "feet" on bag bottom and attach with heavy-duty snap set tools. A shoe repair or upholstery service may do this for you, if you do not have the equipment.

"Having lost luggage more than once, I always begin a trip with carry-ons only. I developed this not-so-little case to fit within my carry-on bag. I may pack it folded up and empty, but it always comes home full!"

103

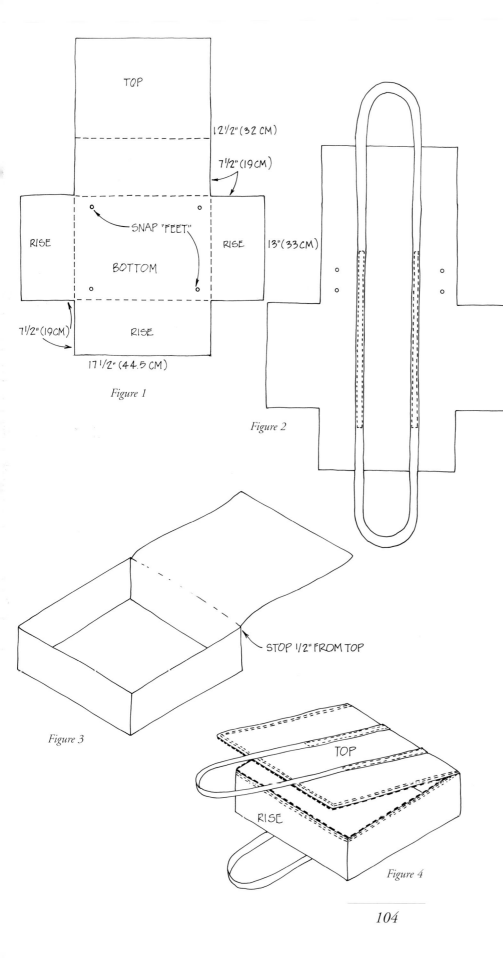

TOP

12 1/2" (32 CM)

7 1/2" (19 CM)

SNAP "FEET"

RISE

RISE

RISE

13" (33CM)

BOTTOM

7 1/2" (19CM)

RISE

17 1/2" (44.5 CM)

Figure 1

Figure 2

STOP 1/2" FROM TOP

Figure 3

TOP

RISE

Figure 4

4. Cut approximately 96" (2.5 m) of seatbelt strap or nylon webbing and lay down on the bag. See Figure 2. Adjust length of straps as desired.

5. Keeping bag top free, topstitch webbing to outside of bag back, bottom, and front. Stitch close to both edges of webbing, reinforcing at each end.

6. With right sides together, stitch corners along seamline and again 1/4" (6 mm) away. On the two corners that meet the top of the bag, stop 1/2" (1.25 cm) from the top. See Figure 3.

7. Cut zipper to 44" (112 cm). Mount slides at each end so they will meet in the middle when zipped; secure with a folded piece of fabric stitched over the ends. See Figure 2 on page 109.

8. Open the zipper and begin sewing one edge to bag, from one corner of the top, around to the opposite corner. See Figure 4. Stitch slowly, hand-turning the sewing machine wheel at the corners if necessary. Stitch again 1/4" (6 mm) away.

9. Sew the remaining zipper edge to the top edge of the "rise" or side panel. Stitch again 1/4" (6 mm) away.

10. To fold the case for packing, push the front rise into the bottom, push the sides in, push the back rise down, and wrap the top around the case like the flap of an envelope.

THREE-POCKET TRAVEL TOTE

Designed by Ronke Luke-Boone

A beautifully-made tote bag will mean more to you than any store-bought, and it can be customized to meet your individual travel needs, from casual cotton to dressy suede.

Materials and Tools

▶ 1 yd (.95 m) of 54" (137 cm) fabric of choice (this is enough for both the outer bag and lining). Suggested fabrics include heavy weight ethnic prints, mud cloth, home furnishing fabrics, linen, canvas, burlap, and lightweight leather or suede.

▶ ¼ yd (.25 m) of 54" (137 cm) contrasting fabric, for outer pocket

▶ ½ yd (.5 m) medium- to heavy weight fusible interfacing

▶ 2½ yds (2.3 m) of 2" (5 cm) cotton webbing for straps

▶ 1½ yds (1.4 m) contrasting or matching piping (optional)

▶ 9" (23 cm) heavy-duty zipper

▶ 16" (40.5 cm) heavy-duty zipper

▶ Lightweight batting, for lower pocket (optional)

▶ Lightweight foam, for bag front and back (optional)

▶ Cardboard

▶ Decorative beads or tassels of choice

Designer Tip

▶ I like to add the batting to the lower pocket and foam to the front and back. They give the bag a soft feel, but they also provide support so the sides are always upright and the pocket doesn't droop.

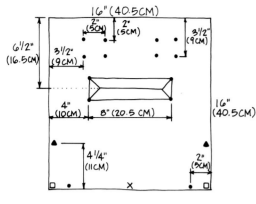

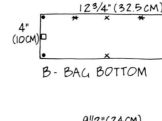

B - BAG BOTTOM

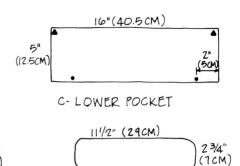

C - LOWER POCKET

A - BAG / LINING FRONT & BACK

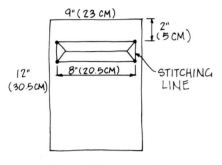

D - ZIPPER POCKET

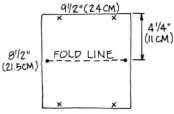

E - INSIDE POCKET

F - CARDBOARD INSERT

Pattern Pieces

A - Bag/Lining Front and Back: cut four from primary fabric and two from interfacing

B - Bag Bottom: cut four from primary fabric and two from interfacing

C - Front Lower Pocket: cut two

from contrast fabric and one from interfacing

D - Zipper Pocket: cut one from contrast fabric and one from interfacing

E - Inside Pocket: cut one from contrast fabric and one from interfacing

F - Cardboard Insert: cut as many as needed for a firm base

Instructions

NOTE: Seam allowances are ¼" (6 mm).

RS = Right Side; WS = Wrong Side

1. Fuse interfacing to the wrong side of all outer bag and pocket pieces, and transfer markings.

2. On one of the two interfaced Front/Back A pieces, baste along the center line and ends of the zipper markings. Repeat on Zipper Pocket D.

3. With right sides together, pin Zipper Pocket D to bag front, matching symbols and basted lines. Stitch along stitching lines, pivoting at small dots at the corners. Slash along center line, which you marked with basting, stopping ½" (1.25 cm) from end. Clip diagonally to small dots; do not clip through stitching. See Figure 1. Turn pocket to inside and press. You have just made the zipper opening.

4. Shorten 9" (23 cm) zipper to fit underneath opening. Center zipper opening over zipper, baste, and stitch in place. See Figure 2.

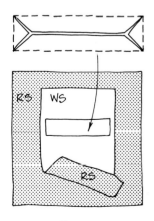

Figure 1

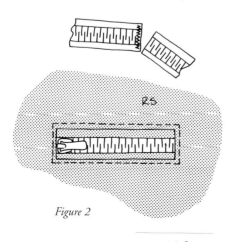

Figure 2

Figure 3

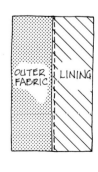

Figure 4

5. Fold pocket D in half, right sides together. Stitch around three edges to form the pocket bag, taking care not to catch the bag front. See Figure 3.

6. If piping lower pocket, baste to one long edge of Pocket C along seamline.

7. With right sides together, stitch lower pocket sections together along one long edge, over optional piping. Press seam allowance toward non-interfaced pocket and understitch seam allowance to non-interfaced side.

8. Fold lower pocket in half lengthwise, matching raw edges; press; baste three unfinished edges closed. If desired, encase a layer of batting inside pocket before basting, to give the pocket a soft touch.

9. Matching dots and triangles, baste Pocket C to bag front along sides and bottom. See Figure 5.

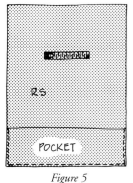

Figure 5

10. Reinforce lower edge of front and back by stitching through dots along seamline, using a very small stitch; clip to dots. You will be reinforcing the front through both the bag and pocket layers. See Figure 6.

11. Cut the cotton webbing in half. Turn under each end ½" (1.25 cm),

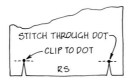

Figure 6

and stitch to bag front and back where marked by dots. See Figure 7.

12. Shorten 16" (40.5 cm) zipper to fit top edge of bag within seam allowances. With right sides together, stitch one long edge of zipper to top edge of front, and other long edge of zipper to top edge of back.

Figure 7

13. With right sides together, stitch bag back to front at side seams; press seams open.

14. If piping bag bottom, baste to right side of Bag Bottom B along seamline, clipping piping seam allowance to pivot around corners.

15. With right sides together, pin Bottom B to lower edge of bag, matching dots, X's, and squares. Stitch, pivoting at corners.

16. Fold Inside Pocket E in half, right sides together; stitch side and top edges, leaving open between X's. Turn right side out, press, and baste across opening. See Figure 8.

Figure 8

17. Edgestitch pocket to the right side of one bag lining piece where desired.

18. With right sides together, stitch side seams of front and back lining (or inside bag pieces); press seams open.

19. Pin lining bottom to lower edge of bag lining (or inside bag), matching dots, X's, and squares. Stitch both short edges and one long edge, pivoting at dots. Leave other long edge open between *'s.

20. With right sides together, insert outer bag inside lining, and stitch around upper edge.

21. Turn to right side through opening in lining; press, and topstitch close to zipper. Optional: Insert foam into bag front and back, through opening in lining before topstitching.

22. Neatly slip stitch opening in bag lining closed.

23. With right sides together, stitch remaining bottom pieces together around three sides, leaving open between *'s; turn right side out, and press.

24. Insert cardboard piece(s) and slip stitch opening closed. Insert bottom into bag.

25. Adorn zipper pulls with beads, tassels, or other decoration of your choice.

26. Pack up, and happy trails!

VINTAGE PACKING PANACHE

Designed by Susan Hart Henegar

*P*rotect your vintage luggage with a custom cover that also provides some extra packing space. Then make the fold-flat tote on page 103 to fit inside, ready to carry your on-the-road purchases.

Materials and Tools

▶ 1¾-2 yds (1.6-1.85 m) rubberized vinyl, backed taffeta, canvas, or auto convertible top fabric

▶ 1½ yd (1.4 m) heavy duty zipper (4.5 coil) and two zipper slides or pulls

▶ Two twist toggles (shown here), buckles, snaps, or hook-and-loop dots

▶ Four large commercial grade snaps for "feet" (optional)

▶ Measuring and marking tools

▶ Awl

▶ Sewing machine needles appropriate for leather, size 18 or 20

▶ Heavy duty quilting or nylon thread

Instructions

NOTE: Custom cover shown here was made for a suitcase measuring 13" x 18" x 6" (33 x 45.5 x 15 cm).

"I love vintage fashions and therefore enjoy traveling with the classy luggage of past times. However, the older cases often need some protection, so this custom-fitting cover does the job. It also provides extra carrying capacity, including space for a fold-flat satchel that I can use for bringing home my purchases. With the cover and the fold-flat satchel, I have all the gear I need and can travel both ways with only carry-on luggage. Both bags fit easily on my indispensable wheeled cart."

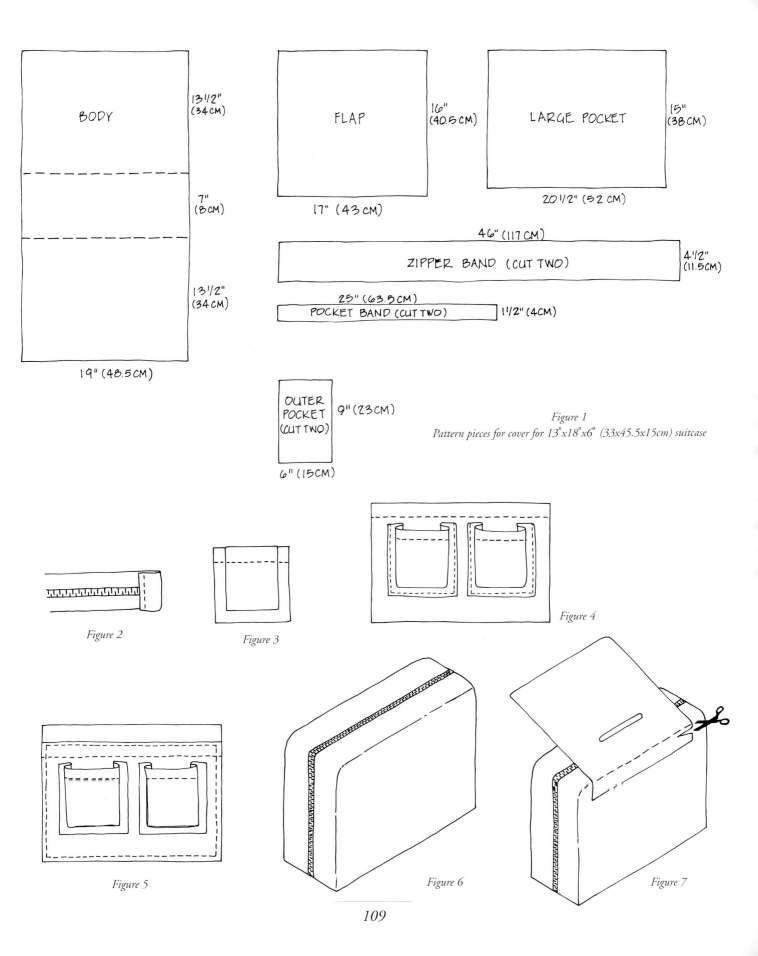

BODY

13½" (34CM)

7" (8CM)

13½" (34CM)

19" (48.5CM)

FLAP

16" (40.5CM)

17" (43 CM)

LARGE POCKET

15" (38CM)

20½" (52 CM)

46" (117CM)

ZIPPER BAND (CUT TWO)

4½" (11.5CM)

25" (63.5CM)

POCKET BAND (CUT TWO)

1½" (4CM)

OUTER POCKET (CUT TWO)

9" (23CM)

6" (15CM)

Figure 1
Pattern pieces for cover for 13"x18"x6" (33x45.5x15cm) suitcase

Figure 2

Figure 3

Figure 4

Figure 5

Figure 6

Figure 7

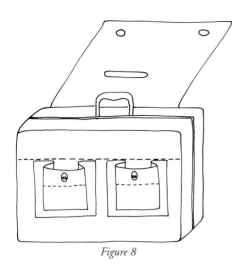

Figure 8

1. Lay out and cut the pieces shown in Figure 1, adding seam allowances.

2. Cut zipper to 46" (117 cm); mount one slide at each end so they will meet in the middle when zipped; secure with a folded piece of fabric stitched over the ends. See Figure 2.

3. Stitch one pocket band around three sides of each pocket; turn top edge under 2" (5 cm) and stitch. See Figure 3.

4. Turn top edge of large pocket under 2" (5 cm) and stitch. Position banded pockets on large pocket, and stitch raw edges of bands in place; stitch again, and trim close to stitching. See Figure 4.

5. Machine baste large pocket to front of suitcase cover, remembering to leave a seam allowance at the top of the suitcase cover. See Figure 5. Sew a tiny tuck at bottom corners, so the pocket will stand away from the cover.

6. Sew zipper band to each edge of zipper, leaving teeth exposed. Sew zipper assembly to three sides of

the cover, turning corners carefully. See Figure 6.

7. Determine the position of your suitcase's handle and mark the position on the cover flap piece. Cut a hole in the flap large enough to easily slip over suitcase handle and topstitch several rows around hole.

8. Position the flap on the back side of the suitcase cover so that it will securely cover the tops of the front pockets; topstitch in place and trim close to stitching. See Figure 7.

9. Position twist toggles or other closures and mount on pocket tops and flap front, using the awl to make a starter hole. See Figure 8. The cover

will zip closed to each end of your suitcase's handle, and the flap will hold everything in securely.

10. Apply optional snaps to bottom as "feet," using heavy-duty snap set tools. A shoe repair or upholstery service may do this for you, if you do not have the equipment.

Designer Tips

▶ Vintage luggage is often a bit smaller than our modern travel cases, which makes it perfect for carry-on travel. This custom cover provides enough additional packing space, for reading materials, business files, and even a raincoat, that I don't mind the smaller size. Besides, with these handy exterior pockets, I don't have to get inside the carry-on bag just to grab a book.

▶ Commercial rubberized fabrics are great for this cover, because nothing frays. You can topstitch very close to the edge, for a professional-looking finish.

▶ I cut my zipper bands and zippers a little longer than needed, and trim as I stitch. Then I'm sure I won't run short before I get all the way around the cover.

A RECORD OF ONE'S JOURNEYS

Designed by Julie Crabtree

*O*ne of the best parts of traveling is bringing home memories of your adventures. These beautiful journals will be a special place to record all you saw and did.

Materials and Tools

▶ Medium weight cotton print fabric or custom fabric of your own design (see Designer Tip below)

▶ Lightweight fleece

▶ Stabilizer of choice

▶ Heavyweight fusible interfacing

▶ Interesting paper for inside cover of journal

▶ Variegated rayon embroidery thread

▶ Sewing thread to match or coordinate with print fabric

▶ Embroidery floss in coordinating colors

▶ Cord in coordinating color or plain string, ⅛" (3 mm) diameter, at least 2 yds (1.85 m) long

▶ Paper of choice for inside pages

▶ Tailor's chalk

▶ Fabric glue

▶ Hook-and-loop dots, ½" (1.25 cm) diameter

"Taking a journal along on vacation should be as natural as packing a camera. You can describe your experiences, make sketches of what you see, and collect keepsakes from everywhere you go. Once you get back home, your journal will evoke lots of pleasant memories."

- Metalfil or embroidery sewing machine needle
- Machine darning foot (optional)
- Stiletto or awl, for making holes in journal cover for lacing
- Hole punch

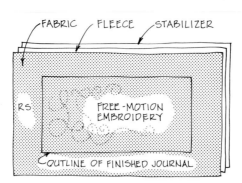

Figure 1
Making the journal cover

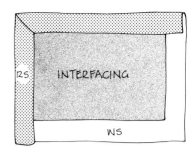

Figure 2
Folding under edges

Instructions

1. Cut rectangles of fabric, fleece, and stabilizer several inches larger than the desired finished size of the journal. For example, if the finished journal is to be 7" (18 cm) tall and 10" (25.5 cm) wide when open, cut the fabrics 11" x 14" (28 x 35.5 cm). The excess fabric provides stability while stitching the free-motion embroidery and also allows for turning around the edges of the journal.

2. Make a fabric sandwich with the cotton print on top (right side up), fleece in the middle, and stabilizer on bottom; pin together. Mark the outline of the journal size with tailor's chalk on the cotton print.

3. Set sewing machine for free-motion embroidery, according to your owner's manual, and thread with variegated rayon.

4. Drop feed dogs, release presser foot, and begin to sew in a random pattern, slowly guiding the fabric with your hands. Gradually fill as much of the traced outline as desired. See Figure 1.

5. To add texture, wind all six strands of the embroidery floss on the bobbin by hand; loosen the bobbin tension screw to allow the thicker thread to pass through the bobbin case. Thread the machine on top with regular sewing thread.

6. Turn the fabric sandwich wrong side up, so stabilizer is on top, and slowly stitch in a circular motion, guiding the fabric with your hands as above. Work slowly and in small areas.

7. Return machine and bobbin settings to normal. With plain thread in the bobbin and the rayon variegated thread on top, use a zigzag stitch to fill in areas as desired, working on the right side.

8. Pull all thread tails to wrong side and tie off.

9. Trim stabilizer and fleece along traced outline or to desired finished measurements.

10. Cut the interfacing to finished journal measurements and fuse to wrong side of journal, according to manufacturer's directions. NOTE: If you cannot find a heavyweight fusible interfacing, purchase a non-fusible and apply with fabric glue.

11. Trim excess fabric to 1½" (4 cm) all around traced outline; fold under and glue to interfacing. Trim and miter corners. See Figure 2.

12. Cut a piece of lining paper several inches larger than journal cover; glue to wrong side. Don't trim paper to finished size until glue is dry.

13. To finish edges, cut store-bought or custom cord several inches longer than outside measurement of journal; dab one end with glue and let dry. To make your own custom cord, see Designer on page 114.

14. Starting at the bottom center of the journal and using a wide zigzag stitch, gradually sew the cord to the edge of the journal. Be sure the stitches are wide enough to go over the cord and through the journal. At the corners, gently turn the journal by hand and stitch slowly, making sure the cord stays close to the journal edge. See Figure 3.

15. When you are within 1½" (4 cm) of the starting point, trim the remaining cord to overlap a bit; dab the end with glue and let dry. Continue to zigzag the remaining cord to the end, backstitching a few times to secure the overlapped ends.

This pretty hand-painted journal is the perfect companion on a nature trip. The designer used acrylic paints for the wild flowers and then free-motion quilted only the background, so that the painted forms would stand out in relief. If you're uncomfortable with painting or drawing, create the same nice impression with appliqué: cut shapes out of coordinating fabrics, fuse them to the journal cover, and stitch around them in the same way.

Before you head out the door, stash your journal, sunglasses, and art supplies in the matching tote (below right). You'll still have room to stow any treasures you find along the way. It's easy to make: machine quilt and embroider a square of fabric to match the journal cover and attach to a simple lined bag with a drawstring. Stitch different sized pockets to the inside of the bag, to safely hold pencils, glasses, car keys, and other necessaries.

It's fun to create your own custom-printed journal cover (far right) by pressing fabric onto acrylic paint dabbed on a glass surface. For a marbleized effect, trail a toothpick or pencil tip through the dabs of paint before applying the fabric. When dry, embellish the fabric with machine embroidery, beads, and other beauties.

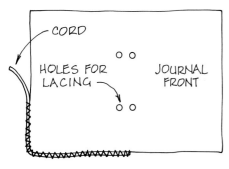

Figure 3
Attaching cord to edges

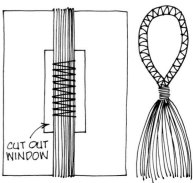

Figure 4
Making tassels

16. To make the front fastener, trim and glue end of leftover cord. Wrap into a ½" (1.25 cm) coil, hand stitching the rows as you go. Leave a tail of about 1½" (4 cm); trim and glue end.

17. Position the tail as desired on the back cover of the journal and zigzag end in place. Glue a hook-and-loop dot to back of coil.

18. Glue the corresponding hook-and-loop dot to front cover, to meet the coiled fastener.

19. Cut another piece of cord for lacing through the journal and inside pages; trim ends, then glue.

20. For the inside pages, cut paper rectangles a little smaller than the journal measurement; cut as many as desired, depending on the weight of the paper you choose. Fold each rectangle in half. Determine placement of holes and punch with hole punch.

21. Place a punched page on front of journal and mark hole placement; repeat on back. Use the stiletto or awl to make holes through journal cover big enough for lacing cord.

22. Place pages inside journal and start lacing cord through one of the holes in the front cover; thread through corresponding holes in pages, through the back, and return to front in the same manner.

23. Knot the lacing, allowing enough ease for the pages to lie flat when the journal is open. Make a loop in each end of the lacing and zigzag securely; trim any stray ends. Add a tassel through the loop. See Figure 4.

Make a template for a tassel with an index card or rectangle of lightweight cardboard; cut a window out of the middle of the card, long enough for the tassel loop. Wind desired threads around the template and stitch over the threads in the cut-out window with a narrow zigzag. Clip the tassel ends and remove from template. Thread tassel through the end loop of the journal's lacing; fold tassel in half and wrap tightly with thread, leaving unstitched ends hanging free.

Designer Tips

▶ Before you begin the free-motion embroidery on your journal, spend some time experimenting on scraps of fabric to get the feel for the stitching and to determine the best machine settings.

▶ For the journal's edging and lacing cord, you can buy readymade or make your own on the sewing machine. To do this, hold a piece of string under the presser foot and lower the feed dogs. Choose a wide enough and short enough zigzag to cover the string, and slowly feed the string through. If the stitching doesn't completely cover the string, feed it through a second time. If you change thread colors each time you pass the string through or move the string at different speeds, you'll get wonderfully varied color combinations.

▶ Feel free to experiment with different papers for the inside cover and pages. There are so many interesting sheets available at print shops and art supply stores.

Velvet Evening Bag

Designed by Lisa Sanders

This easy-to-pack elegant little bag helps you look really dressed up, even if you leave your best jewelry back home.

Materials

▶ Piece of velvet, 12" by 16" (30.5 by 40.5 cm)

▶ Strip of corded and beaded lace, approximately 3" by 16" (7.5 by 40.5 cm)

▶ Lining fabric of choice, 12" by 16" (30.5 by 40.5 cm)

▶ 7" (18 cm) zipper

▶ 1½ yd (1.4 m) decorative cord for handle

▶ Two tassels

Instructions

NOTE: Seam allowances are ½" (1.25 cm).

1. Arrange lace strip on velvet as desired, and pin or baste in place. Hand stitch to velvet invisibly, along outer edge of strip.

2. Fold velvet in half, right sides together, matching the 12" (30.5 cm) edges; baste along seamline. Center zipper along seamline and sew in place, stitching beyond each end of the zipper ½" (1.25 cm), leaving the remaining seam open. See Figure 1.

3. Stitch the ends of the decorative cord to the open seam at the beginning and end of the zipper. See Figure 2.

4. Stitch the remaining seam closed. You will now have a tube shape.

5. Gather each open end with a basting stitch and tack seam allowances to the inside. See Figure 3.

6. Insert cord end of tassel into each gathered end and secure with several hidden stitches. Open zipper, turn bag inside out, and secure gathered ends again with several stitches in the seam allowance.

7. With wrong sides together, stitch the lining along the 12" (30.5 cm) edges, leaving an opening in the middle approximately 6½" (16.5 cm) long to accommodate the zipper. Press seam open; gather the open ends and secure with stitches.

8. Insert lining into bag, wrong sides

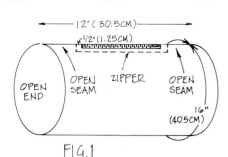

FIG.1

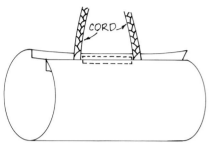

FIG.2

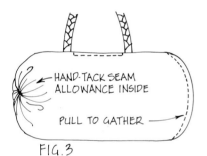

HAND-TACK SEAM ALLOWANCE INSIDE

PULL TO GATHER

FIG.3

together, and pin along the inside zipper opening seam allowance. Close the zipper to be sure that the lining stays clear of the bag opening; if necessary, adjust lining.

9. Turn the bag inside out and slip stitch lining to bag along the zipper opening seam allowances.

10. Tack gathered ends of lining to seam allowances of gathered bag ends. Turn bag right side out.

Designer Tips

▶ You can attach any type of lace or decorative trim to the bag, but the cording on this lace strip provides a conveniently firm outline to support the hand stitches.

▶ If you're going to take this bag as an evening accessory during your trip, put it to work on the way to your destination as a protective tote for hose, jewelry, or other delicates. Packing something inside will also keep the bag from getting crushed and wrinkled in your luggage.

JEWELRY
Designed by Susan Hart Henegar

Whether it's costume jewelry or the real thing, your valuables deserve to be protected in this classy holder made from vintage fabric.

Materials and Tools

▶ ¼ yd (.25 m) fashion fabric

▶ ¼ yd (.25 m) fabric for lining

▶ ¼ yd (.25 m) clear heavyweight plastic

▶ 3 yds (2.75 m) grosgrain ribbon, ⅜" (1 cm) wide

▶ ¼ yd (.25 m) soutache braid

▶ ¼ yd (.25 m) fusible web

▶ Fray retardant

Instructions

NOTE: Jewelry roll-up shown here measures 15" x 9" (38 x 23 cm).

1. Cut fabric, lining, and fusible web a bit larger than desired finished size of roll-up.

2. Cut piece of plastic a bit larger than size of fabrics cut in step 1.

3. Lay a piece of soutache across the middle and stitch down through all layers. See Figure 1.

4. Fold the plastic on each side of the stitched soutache in half and cut

ROLL-UP

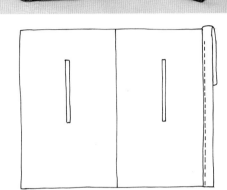

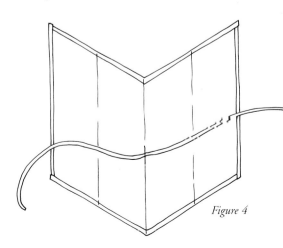

Figure 3

6. Place the ribbon along the next edge, tucking the end under the unstitched portion of the previous ribbon; fold over the top, as before, and stitch through all layers, leaving ½" (1.25 cm) unstitched at far end. Repeat with two remaining edges.

7. Topstitch a second row around all four edges.

8. Sew remaining ribbon on the outside of the roll-up, as a tie. See Figure 4.

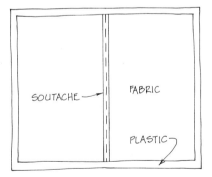

SOUTACHE → FABRIC

PLASTIC

Figure 1

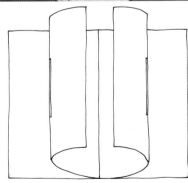

Figure 2

Figure 4

a vertical slit along the foldline. See Figure 2. Lay plastic back down on fabric, baste around edges, and trim even with fabric layers.

5. Place the grosgrain ribbon along one short edge of the fabric rectan-

gle, folding it over the top, and bringing it down the back side; trim even with fabric. Stitch to fabric through all layers, from starting point to ½" (1.25 cm) from end. See Figure 3.

LUGGAGE HELPERS

Designed by M. Luanne Carson

Whip up a family of assorted bags and totes that keep your assorted wardrobe items organized. Soft and washable fabrics are practical, while clear plastic lets you see what's inside.

Construction Notes From the Designer

▶ It's amazing how handy these assorted luggage helpers are when you're traveling, for organizing small items, protecting shoes and belts, or for keeping soiled laundry separate from clean. Choose lightweight, washable fabrics and cut rectangles of any size you desire; sew around three sides with French seams or bind the edges with a sheer nylon seam finishing tape to eliminate raveled threads.

▶ Make a narrow casing for an elastic or ribbon drawstring in some bags, and insert a zipper in others. For a larger bag, like the traveling dresser drawer shown here, sew a self-fabric strip to the top and bottom rectangles to form sides; the width of the strip determines the depth of the finished bag. You can insert a zipper in the center strip or insert two zippers pointing toward each other in the seam between the strip and the top; when unzipped, the top folds back out of the way just like a soft suitcase.

▶ A larger, zippered bag serves as a traveling dresser drawer for lingerie and other small garments. I pack it softly at home, so it can fit over the other items in my suitcase. When I arrive at my destination, I simply lift it out of the suitcase and put it right into the hotel room dresser. It keeps related or small contents together, so I never have to search through my luggage for a particular item.

▶ The clear plastic bag is perfect for small accessories, because you can see everything at a glance. When sewing, use a long stitch to avoid perforating the plastic to the extent that it separates into two pieces. To help the plastic move easily when stitching, use a Teflon-coated presser foot or layer the plastic between sheets of tissue paper or tear-away stabilizer.

This custom-made sewing toolkit is easy to pack, takes up little room, and has everything you will need to fix up a garment mishap.

Materials and Tools

▶ Fabric scraps for inner and outer layers of kit

▶ Lightweight fleece or batting

▶ Lingerie elastic

▶ Ribbon or other closure, such as buttons or hooks and eyes

▶ Items for mending kit

▶ Cutting and marking tools

Instructions

NOTE: Mending kit shown here measures 7½" x 21½" (19 x 54.5 cm).

1. Select inner and outer fabrics, ribbons, and trims, as desired.

2. Assemble necessary mending items; place items on fabric in desired arrangement.

3. Mark placement for elastic to hold mending items as arranged; mark size of kit needed to hold all items.

4. Remove mending items and set aside; cut inner and outer fabrics to

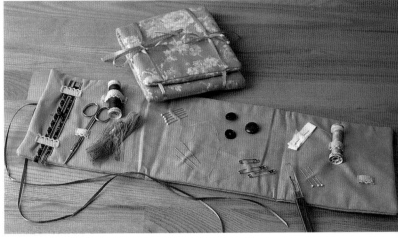

size, including seam allowances; cut two layers of fleece to same size as fabric.

5. Cut elastic pieces required to hold mending items in place; stitch to markings on inner fabric piece, using matching or contrasting thread and plain or decorative stitching, as desired.

6. Baste fleece to wrong side of each fabric piece; if using ribbon as kit closure, cut to desired length and baste to wrong side of one fabric piece at seamline.

7. With right sides together, stitch around outside edge of kit, leaving an opening for turning. Be sure that basted ends of ribbon are caught in the seam. Trim seam allowances, turn right side out, and press. Slip stitch opening.

8. Insert mending items, fold kit into thirds, and tie closed with ribbon.

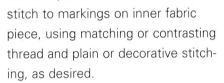

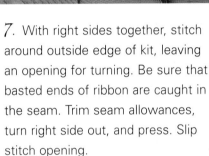

Designer Tip

▶ Select the mending items you need to carry with you before deciding on the size of the kit. Then make the kit to fit the items so it won't take up any extra space in your luggage. If you need only a threaded needle, seam ripper, and spare button, make a very small kit and embellish it so you can wear it as a pin. No one will know that your creative jewelry is also a toolkit.

SHOE PROTECTORS
Designed by Lisa Sanders

Keep your shoes, and the other clothes in your luggage, well-protected with these easy-to-make shoe bags. The soft fabric bag is gentle on fancy shoes, and the clear plastic panel in the nylon bag lets you see at a glance which shoes you packed.

FABRIC SHOE BAG

Materials

▶ Piece of soft fabric, 11" by 26" (28 by 66 cm)

▶ Thread to match

Instructions

NOTE: Seam allowances are ½" (1.25 cm).

1. With right sides together, fold fabric in half, matching 11" (28 cm) edges. Stitch each side. Finish seam allowances with serger or zigzag stitch.

2. Press top edge of bag under ¼" (6 mm); fold under ½" (1.25 cm) and stitch ⅜" (1 cm) from folded edge.

3. Turn right side out and press.

SEE-THROUGH NYLON SHOE BAG

Materials

▶ ⅓ yd (.3 m) nylon fabric

▶ Piece of clear plastic fabric or shower curtain, 4" by 10" (10 by 25.5 cm)

▶ 12" (30.5 cm) elastic, ½" (1.25 cm) or ⅜" (1 cm) wide

▶ Thread to match

▶ Tissue or other paper

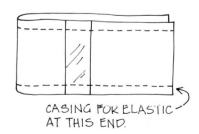

CASING FOR ELASTIC AT THIS END.

Instructions

NOTE: Seam allowances are ½" (1.25 cm).

1. Cut the fabric into two rectangles: 10" by 19" (25.5 by 48.5 cm) and 10" by 10½" (25.5 by 26.5 cm).

2. Sew the clear plastic to the 10" (25.5 cm) edge of the large rectangle and the 10" (25.5 cm) edge of the small rectangle. If the plastic sticks in your sewing machine, lay a piece of paper over the seam and sew through it; then, tear the paper away.

3. Turn seam allowances toward the nylon fabric and topstitch ¼" (6 mm) from seam. You may need to use the paper again.

4. Fold this large fabric/nylon rectangle in half, right sides together, and stitch sides. See illustration. Finish seam allowances with serger or zigzag stitch.

5. To make casing for elastic, turn under top edge ¼" (6 mm) and stitch. Turn under again 1" (2.5 cm) and stitch ⅞" (2.2 cm) from folded edge, leaving a small opening. Turn bag right side out.

6. Insert elastic into casing through opening. Pull it to desired tightness, overlap ends, and stitch through and through.

7. Stitch opening in casing closed.

Designer Tip

▶ Choose the fabric for your shoe protectors depending on the types of shoes you'll be taking. Soft fabrics are gentle on dressy shoes for fancy occasions, while the nylon protects the other items in your suitcase from dirt and moisture on walking boots and shoes.

PACK-FLAT HAT

Designed by Jeff Quattrone

*D*on't leave your favorite millinery fashions at home because they won't pack into your suitcase. Instead, make this cool open-top hat that is easy to pack and wear.

Materials and tools

▶ ½ yd (.5 m) buckram

▶ ½ yd (.5 m) heavyweight non-fusible interfacing

▶ ½ yd (.5 m) each of two coordinating fabrics

▶ Measuring and marking tools

Instructions

1. With a tape measure or piece of string, measure the circumference of your head at the level the hat will sit. Most "one size fits all" hats are made for a head circumference of 22" (56 cm), which is considered "medium."

2. Take the measurement and divide by 3.125 (pi) to determine your hat size. For a head circumference of 22" (56 cm), the hat size is 7.

3. For the hat brim, cut a square of buckram 15" x 15" (38 x 38 cm). Cut a square of interfacing 15" x 15" (38 x 38 cm).

4. Measure and cut a 13½" (34 cm) circle from the buckram and mark the center point of the circle.

5. Place the buckram circle in the center of the interfacing square and zigzag close to the edge of the buckram. See Figure 1.

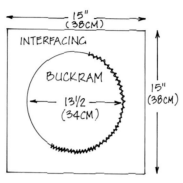

Figure 1

6. Cut a 16" x 16" (40.5 x 40.5 cm) square from each fashion fabric. With right sides together, baste around outside edges and across center line. See Figure 2.

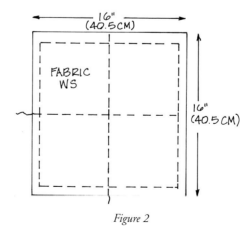

Figure 2

7. Place the interfacing/buckram piece on top of the fabric, buckram side up. From the center point marked on the buckram, measure and mark 7" (18 cm) above, below, and to both sides of the center mark. Repeat at the in-between points, to get a circle that measures 14" (35.5 cm) in diameter. See Figure 3.

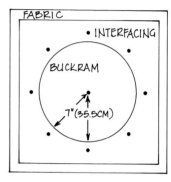

Figure 3

8. Stitch a circle through all layers, from mark to mark. Trim ⅛" (3 mm) away from stitching.

9. In the center of the buckram/fabric circle, mark another circle whose diameter equals the number you arrived at in step #2 (in the hat shown here, this measurement is 7). You may position this second circle at the center of the buckram/fabric square or offset it slightly toward the back if you plan to wear the hat low on the back of your head.

10. Cut out the inner circle and turn the brim right side out; press lightly. You may want to topstitch the outer edge of the brim. Baste raw edges of inner circle (head opening) together; remove all other basting threads.

11. For the sides of the hat, cut a

strip of each fabric that is 1" (2.5 cm) longer than the circumference you measured in step #1 by the desired width. In the hat shown here, the denim was cut 4" (10 cm) wide and the floral print was cut 3" (7.5 cm) wide.

12. With right sides together, stitch fabric strips together along both long edges and one short end. Turn right side out and press flat, matching long seams. See Figure 4.

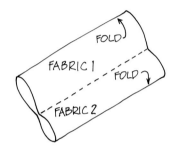

Figure 4

13. Starting from the center back, wrap the narrower side of the two-fabric strip (the floral print in the hat shown here) around the raw edges of the head opening and hand-stitch in place invisibly, through all layers. The wider side of the two-fabric strip (the denim in the hat shown here) will form the hat's sides.

14. Lap the finished end of the two-fabric strip over the unstitched end and hand-stitch in place.

15. From leftover scraps of fabric, stitch small squares or other shapes on three sides. Turn right side out, press flat, and hand-stitch fourth side closed. Lightly hand-stitch these ornamental shapes in place where desired at center back of hat.

Designer Tips

▶ A softly-sculptured hat works better for an accessory you want to pack flat. However, you can get a crisper look with stiff fabrics and by fusing interfacing to the wrong sides of the fabrics before constructing the hat.

▶ This open-top hat is perfect for hot climates because it makes a fashionable statement while allowing your head to breathe.

123

LIGHTS OUT SLEEP MASK

Designed by Doug Campbell

If you have trouble sleeping away from home, whip up this quick and easy mask to help you block out the bright lights of the city or the Arctic sky in June. This makes a great child's project, too!

Materials and Tools

▸ One piece of brown Kraft or grocery bag paper, 6" x 10" (15 x 25.5 cm)

▸ One piece of black wool felt, 6" x 10" (15 x 25.5 cm)

▸ One piece of black satin-like fabric, 6" x 10" (15 x 25.5 cm)

▸ One piece of brightly-printed cotton fabric, 6" x 10" (15 x 25.5 cm)

▸ Soft pencil

▸ Stapler or pins

▸ 16" (40.5 cm) of ¾" (2 cm) black elastic

▸ 4" (10 cm) of ¾" (2 cm) hook-and-loop tape

Instructions

1. For the mask pattern, bring the long ends of the paper together and make a firm crease along the fold.

2. Hold the paper over your eyes, with the crease centered along your nose. You may want to enlist a helper to trace the pattern.

3. Starting at a point on the crease about ½" (1.25 cm) above the center of your eyebrows, trace the outline of the bones around one of your eyes with a soft pencil, keeping an even ½" (1.25 cm) away from the eye socket. You should end up back on the crease about 2" (5 cm) below where you started.

4. Fold the paper in half along the crease, and cut along the traced pencil line.

5. Unfold the paper and hold it back up to your face, to be sure it will cover your eyes completely.

6. Make a fabric sandwich with the satin-like fabric on the bottom, the felt next, the cotton next (pattern side up), and the paper pattern on top.

7. Staple or pin the sandwich together in three or four places to hold the layers together.

8. Cut along the penciled outline of the pattern.

9. Cut the elastic into two 8" (20.5 cm) lengths.

10. Insert one end of each elastic piece about ½" (1.25 cm) into the fabric sandwich at the outer corners of the mask; staple or pin in place through all layers except the paper. Remove the paper pattern and set aside.

11. Hold the mask up to your face and wrap the ends of the elastic around to the back of your head. Make sure the mask completely covers your eyes and blocks out the light.

12. Trim the ends of the elastic so that they overlap by 4" (10 cm).

13. Stitch around all edges of the mask in a zigzag or decorative stitch, avoiding the staples or pins; remove all staples or pins and stitch around again.

14. To secure the mask around your head, stitch hook side of tape to one end of elastic and loop side to the other.

SCENTED TRAVEL PILLOW WITH CASE

Designed by Lisa Sanders

Catch a few winks anywhere with this lightly scented touch of home. This pretty pillow is lightweight to carry and easy to fit in the smallest corner of your travel tote.

Materials and Tools

▸ Piece of velvet or other soft fabric, 12½" by 16" (31.5 by 40.5 cm)

▸ Piece of printed fabric for pillow case, 15" by 19" (38 by 48.5 cm)

▸ Cord for drawstring, 30" (76 cm) long

▸ Polyester stuffing

▸ Handful of dried lavender or other aromatic herb

Instructions

NOTE: Seam allowances are ½" (1.25 cm).

PILLOW

1. Fold velvet in half, right sides together, and stitch along all three cut edges, leaving an opening of approximately 4" (10 cm) in one end. Turn pillow right side out.

2. Stuff a little more than halfway with the polyester stuffing.

3. Using a single scissors blade or knife, slice into the middle of the stuffing to create a small pocket and pour in the lavender.

4. Finish stuffing the pillow to the desired firmness.

5. Slip stitch opening closed.

PILLOW CASE

1. To make the drawstring casing, fold one long edge under ¼" (6 mm) and then again 1¼" (3 cm); stitch close to bottom fold.

2. Fold fabric in half, right sides together, matching the 15" (38 cm) edges, and stitch bag closed along side and bottom, curving out to raw edge at casing and backstitching to secure thread ends. See illustration.

3. Turn bag right side out. Insert cord into casing and knot ends.

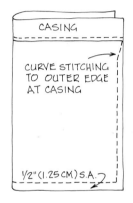

CASING

CURVE STITCHING TO OUTER EDGE AT CASING

½" (1.25 CM) S.A.

JOYCE BALDWIN

is Assistant Professor of Textiles at Western Carolina University in Cullowhee, North Carolina. She passes on her love of fabrics and fashion design to classrooms full of students, and plans periodic student trips to the New York City fashion centers, where she also manages to shop for sewing supplies for her own studio.

KAREN M. BENNETT

lives in Alexander, North Carolina, and has been a member of the Southern Highland Craft Guild since 1983. An energetic woman, she home schools her four children, keeps a large organic garden, and sells her tatting, embroidery, and sewing in galleries and shops. A career highlight was the 1993 commission of a tatted angel for the White House Christmas tree.

JANE BENTON BUTLER

has been using a needle and thread since she was tall enough to see over the sewing machine cabinet, constructing garments ranging from mens' tailored suits to ladies' bathing suits. Her varied career has included stints as manager of a fabric store, parts department manager of a motorcycle shop, and optical frame salesperson. She currently heads an advertising agency, specializing in marketing planning and execution. Jane, who lives in Purcellville, Virginia, especially loves to create three-dimensional items with bead embellishments.

DOUG CAMPBELL

is an architect by profession and enjoys creating solutions to problems, whether it's designing a building, making something in the wood shop, or sewing a camping stuff sack. He emigrated to Asheville, North Carolina from the Rust Belt (i.e. Detroit) in 1980. Travel is an inherited affliction.

M. LUANNE CARSON

thrives on the creative process of integrating fabric and style for unusual effect. She combines her formal training in clothing and textiles with her success as an educator to excite her students about their creative potential. Even after many years at the machine, sewing continues to galvanize Luanne's thoughts and activities. She lives in Arden, North Carolina.

JULIE CRABTREE

has a special interest in developing awareness about machine embroidery as an art. In her varied career, she studied fashion and embroidery in London; raised sheep, Angora goats, and rabbits for their fibers; was an embroidery tutor; and operated a custom sewing business. She has consistently promoted machine embroidery in her own art work and through classes and demonstrations. Julie works in her studio in Twin Lakes, Wisconsin.

JOYCE E. CUSICK

is president of Historic Preservation, Inc., and an architectural historian who prepares Historic District and Individual Building nominations for the National Register of Historic Places. She studied apparel design and construction at Rhode Island School of Design. Joyce, who lives in Dunnellon, Florida, is the author of *Crafting With Lace*, a 1993 Lark/Sterling book.

TRINA L. DROTAR

has had a lifelong love affair with sewing as craft and art. Her wearable art designs have been featured in fashion shows and exhibits, but she also enjoys sewing well-crafted garments for herself. Because her husband is a United Airlines mechanic, Trina is able to travel quite a lot. She lives in Sacramento, California.

FRADELE FELD

has been designing clothes since outfitting her paper dolls as a little girl, and then went on to get a BFA in fashion design. Her first love is clothing, in which she experiments with boldly patterned fabrics and new ways of combining and embellishing them. Her garments have been featured in Fairfield Fashion Shows and other exhibits. Fradele, who lives in Cherry Hill, New Jersey, also teaches and lectures about wearable art, embroidery, and other fabric arts.

DENISE GLICK

is a psychologist, gardener, international folk dancer, and craftsperson who loves sewing and crochet. Her reversible vests and pouches evolved from her love of traveling and the challenge of being efficient and economical. The colors, materials, and designs she chooses are expressions of joy and her love of animals and plants. Denise lives in Asheville, North Carolina.

CATHY HAM

has had a lifelong passion for ethnic textiles and has accumulated a large collection, particularly of knitted textiles, as well as antique knitting, crochet, and other wool-working tools. Self-taught in fiber arts, her recent work combines knitting, crochet, quilting, and embroidery. Cathy was born in Scotland, raised and educated in South Africa, and now lives in Austin, Texas with her husband and four cats, who can often be found in various poses in and around the sewing studio.

CARYL RAE HANCOCK

learned to sew in the 7th grade and went on to make her prom dress and an occasional formal gown, among other things. When she discovered the thrills of machine embroidery and quilting, an addict was born. Now cutting back from a full-time career as an intensive care nurse, she designs, sews, and markets garments and quilts under the name, Cutting Edge Designs. Caryl, who lives in Indianapolis, Indiana, enjoys sharing her addiction for fabric and sewing by teaching classes.

SUSAN HART HENEGAR

is a multi-talented textile artist living in La Jolla, California. She has woven more than 50 tapestries, and has been concentrating on a woven "Travel Series" that explores the ideas of presence and absence. Susan's interest in antique textiles has recently led her to design and produce a line of vintage fabric accessories under the name, HARTLINE.

SONIA A. HUBER

says that taking classes in pattern drafting, after many years of sewing, opened up a new world for her. She has found that time is short for everyone, so making simple changes to a favorite pattern can take it from the realm of "off the rack" to out of the ordinary. Sonia lives in Austin, Texas, and exhibits her work at the Textile Centre of Chicago.

RONKE LUKE-BOONE

has worked with ethnic fabrics for many years and has had her one of a kind fashions featured in *Black Elegance, Essence*, and other national publications. She sells her wearables through the Smithsonian Institution's National Museum of African Art, Smithsonian Museum Catalogue, and other retail outlets. Originally from Sierra Leone, West Africa, Ronke now lives in Fall Church, Virginia, where she operates the travel wear design firm, Serengeti.

ANNE MCCLOSKEY

is passionate about creative sewing and painting, and enjoys inspiring others to try their hands at the projects she designs for books, magazines, and manufacturers. She says the greatest joy in life is the process of making things with her own hands and exploring innovative ways to use colorful, textural materials. Anne lives in Copley, Ohio.

MARY S. PARKER

is descended from a long line of quilters and seamstresses. Her love of sewing and a fondness for cats have remained constant throughout a changing array of professional career positions. Mary lives in Asheville, North Carolina, and recently moved into a larger house with her understanding husband so that she would have sufficient room for her growing fabric stash.

JEFF QUATTRONE

pursues a love of millinery in his studio, Muse on the Loose, named for his approach to art. As he creates each hat, he draws on whatever ideas might be inspiring him at the time, letting the piece take on a life of its own. Jeff, who lives in Philadelphia, Pennsylvania, markets his hats under the name, The St. Clement Collection.

MARY RUSSELL

is a quilt artist living in San Luis Obispo, California. Her wearable quilt art has been featured in various fashion shows and publications. She also is the maker of Double Wedding Ring Rulers, which eliminate the need to trace templates when cutting patches for that quilt pattern.

LISA SANDERS

has worked in all areas of fashion design, including garment design, production management, sales, fabric development, private label development, photo styling, and fashion forecasting for well-known labels such as Christian Dior, Carol Hochman, Victoria's Secret, Kayser, Clifford & Wills, and Macy's. A lover of all things textile, she designs and sews interior decor items, hats and accessories, and clothes for herself, her nieces, and their dolls. Lisa lives in Montclair, New Jersey.

PAT SCHEIBLE

is a decorative painter by trade. She designs and creates with fiber, paint, and most any other material that strikes her fancy. Pat lives in Mebane, North Carolina.

CHAR TERBEEST-KUDLA

learned how to sew when she was five years old and started a long love affair with color, texture, and making useful things from scraps of fabric and thread. She sells her purses, bags, and pocketbooks under the name, Helen's Daughters, at art fairs throughout the upper-Midwest. Char lives in Wisconsin with her goldsmith artist husband.

INDEX

The book and photography crew members take a moment to pose in front of the camper/prop shop/changing room. Seated, left to right: Sandra Stambaugh, Laura Brower, Bob Bowles, Lisa Sanders, Kate Mathews. Standing, left to right: Sarah Tomsky, Kathleen McArthur Mosher, Dana Irwin.